Victory
in the
Valley

Domeka Kelley

ISBN 978-1-64114-210-6 (paperback)
ISBN 978-1-64114-211-3 (digital)

Christian Faith Publishing, Inc.
832 Park Avenue
Meadville, PA 16335
www.christianfaithpublishing.com

Printed in the United States of America

To my amazing wife and best friend, Jessica, and our three
boys and a girl, Bryan, Nakia, Malik,
and Leyah. I dedicate this
book to you all. You watched and endured the storms
And valley experiences with me, which produced this book. I
thank you for your unconditional love and overwhelming
support that anchored me in times when I wanted to give up.
You can be and achieve anything you desire in life always.
Remember, believe in God first and your-
self second. Love you more
every day.

CONTENTS

FOREWORD

April 2, 1978, was the day a child was born. He would be named Domeka K. Kelley. He was raised in a single-parent home, by a mother who loved him dearly and did the best she could to provide for him. He was surrounded by the obstacles of not having his father involved in his life. He went through life with a chip on his shoulder and got himself involved in the streets. Though he made many mistakes, he knew that one day he would become very successful. He would, as some people would say, always have his head in the clouds. He aspired to do things most people thought were impossible. Through his journey in life, he found himself at a crossroad. At that point, he had to make a life-changing decision, which was either to live a life of darkness, or allow God to reveal his light in him.

In the book of John chapter 11, Jesus brings Lazarus back from the dead to life. Jesus calls Lazarus out of the tomb and tells him to come forth. I relate this story to Domeka as he sits at the fork of the road, trying to decide which road to take, when he hears the voice of God. He clearly heard Jesus calling him and ultimately chose to walk with Jesus and answer the call. Life wasn't easy after this decision, but he knew that Jesus was with him, and that gave him great joy.

Isaiah 40:31 states, "They that wait upon the Lord shall renew their strength, they shall mount up with wings as eagles, they shall run and not be weary, and they shall walk, and not faint." I thank God for allowing me to be with you at your lowest state. You're just like an eagle, very protective of their nest and never turning away from the storms life throws your way. I look forward to soaring over the storms with you. See you at the mountaintop!

Jessica Kelley

GREETING

 ello, friends. I thank God through my Lord and Savior Jesus Christ for every one of you who, being led by God, decided to read this book. Psalm 139:16 says, "You saw me before I was born, every day of my life was recorded in your book. Every moment was laid out before a single day had passed." It wasn't by accident you arrived at the decision of picking up this book; it was determined by God well before you blessed this world with your presence that somehow, this book would factor into your life en route to your destiny. God is in control of every detail of our life. Every moment and every action is designed by the mastery of God with purpose. I am overjoyed by the fact your steps are ordered by the Lord. I admire how Apostle Paul began his Epistles and books with powerful confirmations and proclamations such as in the book of Romans, where he makes it clear to its readers that he is first and foremost a servant of Jesus Christ, then an Apostle separated for the furtherance of the Gospel of God. The greeting that I extend to you is directly influenced by Paul's willingness to seize every opportunity to lift up the name of Jesus Christ and be a conduit of His love. Jesus said, "And I, if I am lifted up from the earth, will draw all men to myself." In the context of that statement, Jesus was speaking in reference of his death and resurrection, providing the way of salvation for you and I. That same statement also means to me that if we exalt and magnify Jesus Christ, placing emphasis on him, his works of redemption, and his acts of love, the power of that is so magnetic that it becomes irresistible, and people's desire for him would overtake them, prompting a surge toward him.

I was in a meeting with one of my mentors, a great man of God named Dr. Grant of Liberty Baptist Church in Hampton, Virginia. Dr. Grant asked me what was my dominant spiritual gift, and without hesitation, the word *servant* did a somersault off my tongue as if it was an Olympic diver. I believe the judges gave it a perfect score. Jesus said in Matthew 25:21 (KJV), "His Lord said unto him, well done, thou good and faithful servant: thou hast been faithful over a few things, I will make thee ruler over many things: enter thou into the joy of thy Lord." This profound statement is loaded with promises for the servant by the Savior. Paul, the greatest mind in the New Testament in my opinion, was a servant first. I think I find myself in great company in being a servant for Jesus Christ. *Doulos* is the Greek word for *servant*, which means "a slave, bondman, man of servile condition, one who is completely devoted to another's will while disregarding his own interests."

Dwight L. Moody said, "The world has yet to see what God can do with a man fully consecrated to him, by God's help, I aim to be that man." Moody developed a passion to become a person completely devoted to God, disregarding his own interest and ultimately building one of the greatest Bible institutes in the world. I believe every reader of this book will or already had developed a passion to become completely devoted to the will of God, to accomplish great things for the Kingdom of God. I thank God for His grace, such a blessing being a servant and pastor among His beloved people. Among the promises I have already entered into, joy, by far, is the most prominent in my life. Joy is an expression of the confidence you have in Jesus Christ, understanding God is in control of every detail of your life, leading you to believe that everything will work out for your good. Therefore, instead of worrying about anything, we should praise God for the victory over everything. The purpose of this book is inspired by 1 Thessalonians 3:2–3, where Paul states his purpose for writing the letter to the Thessalonian Church, which was experiencing grave persecution for the Gospel's sake. This church was very young in its faith. Paul had only spent three days with them, and miraculously, the church was planted. Paul's intentions were to strengthen and comfort the people in their faith in hopes that they wouldn't turn away from their faith in the time of afflictions, which we are all appointed to, according to scripture (1 Thess. 3:3).

God has a purpose for this book far greater than the intentions that belong to me. I shared with my wife when I began this book, I said it's as if I am writing with the hand of God. I desire to strengthen and encourage the faith of everyone who reads this book, but I believe God is going to do exceeding abundantly above all that I can ask or think according to the power that's at work in us (Eph. 3:20).

Over the past few years, my family and I have endured what I phrase as "valley experiences," some I will unveil in this book. A valley is defined as a low area or place situated in between mountains and/or hills. In scripture, a valley in many instances is viewed as a low place in comparison to mountains, which are viewed as places of exaltations. Both valleys and mountains, when parallel to life, are considered highs and lows, ups and downs, peaks and valleys. I now understand that whenever I'm in the midst of a low place (valley) in my life, I am simply in between mountains (exaltations). Valleys (lows) in our life are not designed to defeat us; they are temporary holding places preparing us for the mountain (highs), understanding champions are not produced on the mountain but rather celebrated there. Victors, not victims, are produced in the valley. I believe every person at some point in their life experiences a "valley" or low place. I have heard it referred to as "hitting rock bottom." Whatever term you may have used to coin it, I want you to know that difficult time of your life is simply a peek into how great the plans are that God has for your life. Adversity gives birth to a greater sense of accomplishment. Your best days are still ahead of you. I pray that this book brings great joy and confirmation to your heart. Welcome to the "*Victory in the Valley.*"

DOES YOUR STORM

*G*od said, "I am building a greater dependency on me in you, I am increasing your capacity to trust me." There is always more room for you to trust God; never think that you are in a place where you have arrived. I am reminded by the Apostle Paul in 1 Corinthians 10:12: "Wherefore let him that think he stand take heed lest he fall." Paul was eluding to the fact that the children of Israel, after being delivered from Egyptian captivity are under Mose's leadership and teaching day and night, who as the scripture say's drank of that spiritual rock which was Christ. They came to believe that they had arrived spiritually as if they had it all figured out but when the time of testing came in the wilderness, they were overthrown by the lust of the flesh. Paul used them as examples and warnings, reminding us that we will always have room to grow in God, and in our times of testing, we are to remain humble and not prideful, understanding that pride comes before the fall.

Isaiah 26:3–4 says, "Thou wilt keep him in perfect peace who's mind is stayed on thee, because he trust in thee, trust ye in the Lord for ever for in the Lord JEHOVAH is everlasting strength." This scripture immediately came to mind after hearing the Lord declare his intentions for me. Everything was going great in every area of my life at this point. I honestly thought I was trusting God more now than I ever had before. Spiritually I felt whole; the joy of the Lord was very noticeable in my wife and children that oftentimes, it was even contagious. As a family, our faith in Jesus was exemplary. I couldn't resist the notion that God had something more in store for me, but I was a little unsure about the methods he would use to ensure success; therefore, I became a little fearful because I saw in scripture how oftentimes humiliation was before exaltation, and I wanted to be an example of how to get there instead of being a warning. I prayed often, seeking the face of the Lord in this matter, and he lead me to Matthew's Gospel account of Jesus walking on water. I was reassured that all of my concerns would be addressed as the dynamics of the story would unfold, revealing principles and truths that would become paramount to my faith.

After reading Matthew 14:22–33, instantly I became encouraged and excited because I discovered exactly what the Lord wanted me to seek and find. I've read the story numerous times, but never with the revelation had I received on this occasion. The story begins with Jesus commanding his disciples to enter a ship and travel to the other side of the Sea of Galilee while he remained back for prayer after dispersing the possibly fifteen thousand people he fed with five loaves and two fish, the miracle of multiplication. The disciples are now in the midst of the sea, possibly about three or four miles, when all of a sudden, a storm arises and begins to beat against the ship relentlessly. The Sea of Galilee is famously known for its violent storms, which can come up suddenly and be life-threatening for anyone that is in its waters. These storms are caused because of how the Sea of Galilee is situated in the Jordan Rift, with steep hills on all sides. Being seven hundred feet below sea level, it's the lowest freshwater lake on earth. Therefore, the cooler air masses from the surrounding mountains collide with the warm air in the lake's basin. Winds sometimes funnel through the east-west oriented valleys in the Galilean hill country and rush down western hillsides of the lake. The most violent storms, however, are caused by the fierce winds, which blow off the Golan Heights from the east. One such storm in March 1992 sent waves ten feet high crashing into downtown Tiberias and caused significant damage to the city.

Equipped with this information of the Sea of Galilee, I understand how a storm was able to form from out of nowhere and blindside the disciples. Around 3:00 a.m.–6:00 a.m., Jesus, in my opinion, calmly walks on the water toward the disciples, which frightens them even more. They scream out in fear, thinking that it was a ghost. Jesus speaks, "Be of good cheer, it is I."

Peter responds, "Lord if it be thou, bid me to come unto thee on the water."

Jesus said, "Come." What a powerful response from our Lord: "Come."

Peter, being unsure, then steps out on faith, climbs down out of the boat, and for however long, he began to do the impossible. Peter in that moment achieved what no other man had ever done, only Jesus Christ our Lord, who empowered him by the command "Come."

I believe we can reach extraordinary heights even if we're unsure like Peter was, once we respond to the commands of Christ, developing a tunnel vision or focus that allow us to become impervious to the present dangers and distractions. Peter allowed the violent raging of the wind to distract him, and the moment he took his focus off, Jesus he began to sink, being overtaken by fear. Paul reminded Timothy (2 Tim. 1:7) that God didn't give him a spirit of fear, but of power, love, and a sound mind. I believe we forfeit a tremendous amount of blessings that God intends for us to enjoy due to the fact we allow fear to paralyze us. I was assured of the fact that the Lord wanted me to write this book, but I procrastinated because of fear on many levels.

The first of many negative thoughts that discouraged me greatly was "Lord, how am I going to write a book? I'm not an author." I learned that your mind will try and talk your heart out of doing what God purposed you to do by giving you every reason and excuse to why you can't or don't deserve to. The very same day, I shared my idea with my sister in Christ, Ericka "E-money" McSwyne, and God laid on her heart to send me this scripture from Zechariah 4:6: "Not by might, nor by power, but by my spirit, said the Lord of Hosts."

The story of Zerubbabel, the governor of Judah who built the second temple after the Babylonians destroyed Solomon's temple in 587 BC. Zerubbabel was given the sanction to rebuild the temple and return the sacred temple vessels that Nebuchadnezzar II had preserved after the conquest of Babylon. Zerubbabel laid the foundation when the work of building the temple had stalled, and he became discouraged, needing encouragement. The Prophet Zechariah, after seeing a vision, came to him with those prophetic words from the Lord. He told Zerubbabel that he would finish the temple by the Spirit of the Lord and not of his own effort or resources. Zerubbabel was encouraged and continued the work until its completion.

The Lord definitely knows how and when to send comfort and confirmation. Ericka didn't have the slightest inclination that I was struggling with fear and discouragement in that area. Immediately, I knew God was in control, and He would write this book for me. I studied the word *spirit* in Hebrew and Greek, "ruach" and "pneuma," which means "mental disposition, mind, power of God, superhuman." But what stood out among those meanings was the word *breath*. God encouraged and assured me that I would be able to complete this book in "His mental disposition," "His mind," "His power," and by "His breath," making me "superhuman," which means through Him I possess exceptional ability and power. Everything that He "breathes" on comes "alive."

The Bible was written according to 2 Timothy 3:16 by inspiration of God. He "breathed" on men to accomplish His purpose in bringing us His Word in a collection of sixty-six books, which make up the Bible. In like manner, *Victory in the Valley* is inspired by God. I was greatly encouraged and understand that in our moments of despair, just like Peter when we lose sight of God and begin to sink because of fear, remember that Peter shouted, "Lord, save me," and Jesus sprang into action and delivered him. It is the sincere, heartfelt, and outright prayers of desperation that move the heart of God. The moment you realize you can no longer make it on your own, accomplish any task on your own, understanding that you are utterly inadequate without him, he saves you. Having the knowledge that God loves you overpowers the greatest fear or concern that you may have.

I was encouraged by the truth and principles I discovered from this story, but of them all, I want to share the one I deemed most important, especially for the storm I was enduring in my personal life. In verse 32 of Matthews's account of this story, it reveals the moment Jesus entered the ship with the disciples, the wind ceased, which led me to believe the wind knew exactly who Jesus was and, therefore, became subject unto Him. The wind also had knowledge of the fact the disciples were not absolutely convinced of the "Deity of Jesus" as the "Son of God." The wind heard Peter express doubt when he said, "If it be you

Lord." Because of Peter's uncertainty, the wind continued its assault.

I learned a valuable truth from this story, which I was able to practice while being in the most difficult storm of my life thus far. My mother works as a physical therapist assistant, and she does home care as well. One Sunday she brought one of her patients to church with her, an elderly man named Mr. Whittie McCool. He enjoyed the service tremendously, especially the teaching of the Word. He gave my mother a CD to give to me entitled *The Four Spiritual Secrets* by a pastor named Dick Woodward. I thoroughly enjoyed the teaching of Pastor Dick Woodward. I listened to the CD faithfully for about a year. I was absolutely amazed with his knowledge of the Bible and his ability to teach it on a level where anyone could understand.

I was in a meeting one day with a close friend of mine, Mr. Daniel Nice, a devout believer and business mentor to many successful businessmen in my area. I shared with him my excitement about Pastor Dick Woodward, and he just smiled like he normally does, but what he said next would change the landscape of my life forever. He asked me if I wanted to meet him. I said yes, and to my amazement, he called him right then and scheduled a meeting with Pastor Dick Woodward and me. I would spend the next three and half years at his bedside being coached by the most phenomenal, loving person that God has ever created. It started as a mentorship, a seasoned pastor in him developing a young pastor in me, then grew into a father-son relationship. He tenderly referred to me as his beloved son.

Pastor Woodward would become the only earthly father that I would have. My biological father and I never had a relationship, even though we knew one another. I was raised solely by my mother—a strong, determined, intelligent, confident, loving, beautiful woman, who worked three sometimes four jobs to provide for my sister and I. I love my mom. I call her "Suge," short for "sugar," because she's so sweet.

On March 8, 2014, I received some devastating news. Mr. Daniel Nice called me. His voice was low and shaky; he could barely get the words out as he expressed to me that Pastor Woodward had gone to be with the Lord. I fell to my knees, crying inconsolably. I couldn't believe it and didn't want to accept it. I've had close relatives and friends pass, but no one this close to me.

I remember the first day I met him, he asked me a question: "Who are you?" When I responded with my name, then he asked again, "Who are you really?" He had a very special way about him that allowed him to be engaged with a person in such a way while in his presence, you felt like the most important person in the world. You knew that he cared and wanted only the best for you. I am crying right now as I write, just thinking about all the moments we shared. He found a way to crack the codes in my life; he was able to get behind the walls I built for years protecting my heart.

I remember one day while watching Bishop T. D. Jakes, one of my favorite pastors/teachers, I heard him say, "The very walls you've built to protect you from the hurt is the very same wall that's blocking the love from entering in." I battled with rejection, anger, and abandonment, which made me very hesitant to trust and open up to anyone, but yet I felt comfortable with Pastor Woodward. After pouring my heart out to Pastor Woodward, he opened my eyes, and I was able to see there was a little boy inside of me crying out for the affection of his biological father, Andre Rowlett, who had passed away September 1, 2010, after suffering a long battle with cancer, and this little boy never had the opportunity to tell him how much he loved and adored him and how he wished he attended his basketball games to show him how gifted a basketball player he was. Imagining how things might have turned out differently if only he was involved.

I had spent many years resenting my father, only to find out that resentment was just an expression of the love that truly resided in me toward him. My father did something that made me extremely proud and grateful for him. He named me. The Lord placed it in my father's heart to name me Domeka, even though I was involved in a number of fights because of it and on the receiving end of countless jokes. I once had a good friend who was a female whose name was Demica. I was embarrassed by my name growing up, so I went by my middle name Keyell. But now I love it; it's unique, and my name means "belonging to the Lord." I know that I am God's, and I thank him for that. From the very beginning of my life, God had his stamp on me. I was destined to have a relationship with the Lord. Thanks, Pops. I will see you when I get to heaven. Maybe we can finally play that game of one-on-one basketball. I pray that I am making you proud, and I want you to know that I love you more than I ever showed you while you were here.

Pastor Woodward somehow filled that void in my life as much as he could, and all of a sudden, I started growing as a man. Pastor Woodward was a quadriplegic who had already beaten tremendous odds, living past the age of eighty, when the doctors never thought that he would make it that far, but God had work for him still, and he would always tell me that once his work was done, then he would go home to be with the Lord, and I would respond, "Well, I guess you'll be here for quite a while longer because the Lord knows I need you." He would chuckle, and I would cry because I wasn't ready to entertain the thought of not having him tangible in my life.

He counseled me so well, I became accustomed to bringing all of my pastoral questions and concerns, being mindful of not putting too much on him. We established e-mail communications so that our personal home visits would be all about us. I felt confident as a pastor because I knew I had him in my corner; he had all the answers. I began to rely on him more than I relied on God, and that is never good or acceptable. I didn't realize it until after he went to be with the Lord, and God revealed it too. His passing left me in a state of "spiritual depression." I was going through a storm like Peter and the disciples. God spoke again to me: "I am building a greater dependency on Me in you." God wanted to give me a greater capacity to trust Him! God wanted to counsel me, He wanted to be a Father to me, He wanted me to e-mail Him back and forth, and He wanted me to spend intimate times with him on a weekly basis, pouring out my heart to Him.

In the storm that Peter and the disciples endured, the very storm that Jesus walked on water. Jesus said that he constrained them to get on that boat. He made them to get on that boat because it was necessary. If they hadn't gone through that storm, they would have never fully known who Jesus was. If I had not endured the storm of losing Pastor Dick Woodward, I would have never known Jesus the way I know him now. The disciples said, "Now I know that Jesus is the Son of God!" I can say now that I know for sure that Jesus is the Son of God, and Him walking on water shows that he is ultimately in control of every storm that we endure. Jesus being in the boat with the disciples is showing us through his word that he is in the boat with us in our every storm; we have to know it and know him.

Pastor Dick Woodward did an extensive study on eagles. They were his favorite animal. He had a statue of an eagle sitting on a table right next to his bed. My wife called me one day a few weeks after Pastor Dick Woodward had gone to be with the Lord. She said that a huge eagle was flying around our house, and that at one point, it came and rested right on the rooftop. My wife wasn't aware of his fondness for eagles. I started to cry and told her indeed what was taking place. I felt in my heart that eagle was sent by God to encourage me and remind me that Pastor Dick Woodward was still watching over me, even from heaven.

Does your storm know Jesus better than you? Whatever storms you may currently be facing or the ones you will face in the future, understand they are simply present in your life to reveal to you the "Deity of Jesus Christ" as the Son of the living God, and the moment you accept that truth, the sooner the storms subside and eventually are over.

One day Jesus asked Peter and the other disciples a question: "Who do people say that I am?" They responded, "Some say John the Baptist, Elijah, Jeremiah, or one of the prophets." Jesus said, "Who do you say that I am?" He asked this question not before but after they endured the storm in the boat. Peter answered, "Thou art the Christ, the Son of God." Jesus said, "God gave you that revelation."

Scripture teaches that revelation can come via the storms we encounter in life. Storms in life prepare you for the valleys (low places), equipping you with the knowledge of God's Omnipresence. He's with you in every storm, and He's in control of every storm. This storm became the bridge I had to cross over to enter into a place of trusting in the unfailing hands of God. "Your greatest tragedy can become a bridge to your greatest treasure," which is a confident and unwavering trust in God. Welcome to my valley experiences.

VALLEY OF FAMINE

The Bible tells a powerful story about Isaac during a period of famine in the land of Gerar, meaning "lodging place," which was a Philistine town and district in what is today south central Israel, mentioned in the book of Genesis. The Lord appeared unto Isaac during this famine, "drought or shortage," and he told Isaac not to go down into Egypt. In times of severe famine in Palestine, most people went down to Egypt, it was the normal thing to do, but God wanted Isaac to trust in His ability to provide, not to do the natural thing that everyone else would be doing.

During times of drought or difficulties, normally our first course of action is to lean toward what is familiar or what brings immediate relief. Therefore in Isaac's day, many people traveled to Egypt. The Lord told Isaac to stay in the land of Gerar.

Upon reading the story, I tried to put myself in Isaac's shoes or try to imagine what he was thinking when God said that to him. Then I realized how powerful and persuasive the presence of God alone was to Isaac. After being in the very presence of God, I would have been reassured and obedient as well. I am in awe of how hands-on God was in the Old Testament period. His interaction with His people of that day is absolutely phenomenal. That's not to say that God isn't hands-on now, but I do believe to a certain degree that the people of God during those times had a stronger faith than the body of Christ does today. I believe if our faith was as active now as it was then, we would see more miracles being wrought among us.

God told Isaac to remain in the famine land and that He would bless him and give him the entire land. The promises God made Isaac was the covenant He made to Isaac's father, Abraham, and because of Abraham's faithfulness and obedience to God, the oath was extended to Isaac and his descendants. Abraham was a great man of faith, and the Bible says that "Abraham believed God." What a profound legacy Abraham left behind.

When I saw how God blessed Isaac because of his father Abraham's obedience, "generational blessings" came to my mind. I was reminded of the fact that we inherit some blessings of God by the favor that was stored up because of the actions of our parents, grandparents, and family members who served God before us. My grandmother was a devout believer, and there is no doubt in my mind God made her promises that extended to all of her seeds, including myself. I watched my grandmother open her house to strangers. She would take them in, introduce them to Jesus Christ, and become a spiritual mother to them. My grandmother had a passion for souls. She loved people, and I believe that blessing was passed down to me, "generational blessing."

I remember one day my grandmother was having a prayer meeting at her house, and I was sitting on the floor right next to her. I was a little boy at the time, and she said to me, "One day you are going to be a prominent pastor." I looked at her with bewilderment. The very next day, I took a shopping cart from the local grocery store's parking lot and placed a Bible in it and walked up and down the street, telling everyone I was saved and asking people if they wanted to know Jesus, a man who loves us

so much he died for us. I was excited to share his story to anyone who would listen that day. I now understand I was a little
"John the Baptist" preparing the way for "King Jesus," a young
man whose heart at a young age was on fire for Christ, who
wasn't ashamed or afraid to speak in behalf of Jesus.

My aunt Carolyn was amazed by that, so she started taking me on what she called "missionary trips." We would go
throughout the neighborhood, bringing people food and having Bible study and prayer meetings at the homes of anyone
who would have us. I was so excited seeing the smiling faces and
warm receptions of the people who wanted to hear about Jesus.
I love my aunt Carolyn. I am closest to her out of all my uncles
and aunts. I believe it is because of our spiritual connections.
Her zeal for Jesus and passion to serve his people inspired me
tremendously. "Generational blessing" passed down from her
to me.

But as I got older, specifically into my teenage years, my
love for Jesus and witnessing soon became a thing of the past.
I stopped attending church altogether. I started hanging out
with the wrong crowd, associating myself with guys who rarely
came to school, getting kicked out of school, who were involved
in drugs, only concerned with the latest shoes, and dating the
prettiest girls. I thought I was too cool to get involved in anything positive at school. I created an image, developed a reputation completely opposite of how I was raised. I was born to lead
but became a follower.

I absolutely loved the game of basketball. I was very gifted,
talented, and still today my name is mentioned whenever the
debate is made about the best point guard in Newport News,
Virginia. I have become one of those guys who I would hear the
older men in the barbershop refer to as the "could of, would of,

should of guys," all the potential but no drive to overcome all obstacles standing in the way of their destiny. Basketball was a dream I allowed to slip away because I was preoccupied trying to be somebody and something I was not, focused on winning the approval of people who had already given up on themselves, neglecting my true friends who saw my potential wasting away and practically begging me to play basketball.

Dominic Banks, my cousins Jamon "Jada" Green, and Calvin "Squeaky" Chester were my examples, grew up in the same neighborhoods and family, some of the same friends but wouldn't allow anyone to keep them from their destiny, not even me. I was heading down the wrong path fast. In the eighth grade, I was arrested for a concealed weapons charge, and then the summer going into tenth grade, I was arrested again for possession of drugs with the intent to distribute. I spent my entire summer in juvenile detention thinking about my mother and how I was destroying my life. While in detention, I heard a very familiar voice, and at the time, I always contributed the voice to God's voice. He reassured me that in spite of all the wrong I had done, He still loved me, and His plans for my life were irrevocable (unable to change and impossible to revoke). God said, "Look at your mother, and you gain insight of my love. At every court appearance she was there, every visitation day she was there, never judging you, only consoling and loving you."

God said, "Your mother is the epitome of my love for you, a love that's unconditional and unfailing. But my love is greater. I was present at every court appearance and visitation, and even now in this cell I am with you. My love for you is inescapable."

I learned God can enter places and moments in your life where no one else can enter in. He is always there. Whenever I see my mom, I just smile because she is a reflection of God's love, a "generational blessing" from my grandmother to my mom.

My grandmother watched over me. She was deeply spiritual. If you didn't know her, you probably would think she was eccentric, spooky even, but very inspirational and prominent in my life. I remember one occasion my cousin Lindell and I went to a carnival. I was in the eleventh grade at the time. I met a young lady while there, and Lindell said she looked like a younger version of my mom, laughing hysterically. We left the carnival, planned to go out to a night club, but we stopped by my grandmother's house before going. She looked at me and said, "I see blood." I responded sarcastically, "That's the blood of Christ you see, Grandma." Lindell laughed again. She told us not to attend the party because there would be bloodshed, Lindell stopped laughing. My grandmother had our full attention. But what she said next absolutely puzzled me, giving further evidence that she was definitely God's leading lady in my eyes, and from that moment on, I took her seriously. She was very stern, warning me to avoid the young lady I met earlier who looks like my mother because her intentions wasn't good toward me, and she would be detrimental toward my destiny.

Lindell and I both made eye contact instantly, as if one of us told her, and we were trying to figure out which one it was. We didn't attend the party, heeding my grandmother's warning. I woke up the next morning watching the morning breaking news, and the story was about a young man we knew who was gunned down at the same club we were supposed to attend.

My grandmother's influence in my life would be paramount and embraced then after. She warned me on several different occasions, and finally, she said to me with a look of conviction, bypassing my natural man and landing on the ears of my spirit man. My grandmother told me I had a mandate on my life. God needed me now. It was time for me to walk into my destiny, and that if I continued in my ways, God would remove his hand, and destruction would befall me.

I knew it was the Lord speaking through her. I was headed down a road of destruction with some of the things I was involved in and some of the people that I was associated with. Nevertheless, I took heed, understanding the sincerity and urgency. It was on a Thursday, and the following Sunday, I attended Victory Life Church, accepting Jesus Christ in my life.

It was the summer of 2001, the year my friend Michael Vick got drafted to the Atlanta Falcons following a trip from Atlanta were I got to see him play in his first NFL preseason game. While I was in Atlanta, the Lord was dealing with my heart heavily. I recall being at a night club with Michael, my friend Pierre Russell, and a bunch of guys who were with Michael. Some of them were guys we all grew up with. A young lady approached me in the club, and it was odd because she asked me the strangest question, which prompted me to get into my vehicle. Pierre and I, at approximately 1:30 a.m., drove nonstop from Atlanta back home to Virginia. The young lady asked me why and what was I doing in this night club, and she looked at me and said, "You don't belong in here," and I knew it was God using her, and I didn't inform Michael that I was leaving. I just left. I knew God was calling me, and I could no longer run from it. The greatest "generational blessing" handed down to me from my grandmother was the desire to be obedient to God's Word and Commandments.

Abraham, the forefather of faith, walked in obedience to God, passing the "generational blessing" down to Isaac. God told Isaac to remain in the land of Gerar. Scripture says that

Isaac dwelt there. Isaac was obedient to God, regardless of how difficult or impossible his circumstances seemed. The land was not able to produce; therefore, it didn't make sense for a farmer to sow in that dry, hard land in expectation for a future harvest. Scripture states that Isaac sowed in that land and reaped a harvest one hundredfold, meaning that Isaac received one hundred times more than what he sowed. Isaac had faith that God would fulfill his promises. I believe the faith Isaac had was another "generational blessing" he displayed while being prepared to be a human sacrifice unto God.

One day, Abraham, his father, asked him to go along with him to offer a sacrifice unto God, which was nothing outside of the normal. At some point in their journey, Isaac asked his father where was the sacrifice, and his father replied, "God would provide the sacrifice." What Isaac wasn't aware of was that he indeed was the sacrificial offering unto God. Abraham tied Isaac down to the altar. I believe Isaac willfully allowed his father to do so; he humbly surrendered himself to his father. Isaac was essentially saying, "My life is in your hands."

It's been over fifteen years since I surrendered my life to Jesus, saying, "My life is in your hands." Abraham stretched the knife back, determined to sacrifice Isaac. Before he could thrust the knife into Isaac's chest, a voice from heaven called his name twice, getting his attention. "Abraham, Abraham!" the voice shouted.

"Here I am," Abraham replied. He was instructed to look up and see where a ram was caught in the thicket of bushes God provided in the place of Isaac for a sacrifice. Abraham named that place Jehovah-Jireh, meaning "the Lord will provide or see." God will always see to it that he makes a way or provide a "ram in the bush" for his children who operate in faith and obedience. Even when they don't see a way out, God has already prepared a way of escape. God previously promised Abraham not just verbally, but He showed him a vision, and in that vision, God told Abraham to look up toward heaven and count the stars, and if you're able to count them all up, that's how numerous your seed or children shall be.

God further reassured Abraham that it would all begin with Isaac. Abraham believed God not just from what God had told him, but by what God showed him. God placed "vision" in Abraham's heart, which prompted him to trust God for that promise, despite how things had turned out. Abraham was convinced God would fulfill his promise. He believed if he indeed sacrificed Isaac, God would raise him up from the dead to fulfill the promise he made to him. Through Abraham's life, I learned what faith really is. Faith is simply believing God is going to fulfill His word; faith is trusting that God will do exactly what He said he would do. How far are you willing to go or what are you willing to sacrifice to believe God? Abraham was willing to sacrifice his son.

In my "valley of famine," I found myself in a place similar to Abraham's. Isaac was the son that Abraham prayed earnestly for, and God appeared to Abraham and his wife Sarah and promised them that they would give birth to Isaac. Sarah laughed because she knew that she was beyond childbearing age and that it was impossible. I believe God had the last laugh because He told them they would name their son Isaac, which means "laughter." Eventually, God's promise came to pass, and Isaac was born. Scripture says when you delight yourself in the Lord, he will give you the desires of your heart. Abraham desired Isaac, the one thing he wanted in life more than anything else, and yet he was faced with the task of giving it up.

In my "valley of famine" when everything seemed stagnant, nothing growing or producing the fruits I was believing God for, I was faced with the most difficult decision thus far as a pastor. I had to give up the location of where our ministry had been planted for most of our existence. The location had become my Isaac, my promised seed. my wife and I had labored in prayer along with some great members. Ministry in that particular place had become our lives. The Lord by His grace allowed us to turn a used "car lot" into a beautiful edifice and place of worship. So many miracles, lives transformed, families restored, people saved, marriages performed, home goings celebrated, bonds and friendships established, wonderful times and great memories in that place. I envisioned us being there forever. The most difficult decision I had to make was leaving it behind, and it was out of my control. I had to trust the providence of God. Just for a moment, I thought it was all over. I thought I had finished my course. Then God spoke to me. He said, "I close one door only to open another." He further reminded me of the promises He made concerning Psalms Ministries, our church, and suddenly, my "valley of famine" became my "valley of dreams." Just as God told Abraham to look toward heaven and count the stars, He encouraged me to look toward heaven so I could be reminded of the very things He showed me. God gave me dreams, and as long as you have dreams and goals, you have something to reach for or work toward.

I understood that the dream God gave me would lead me from where I was to the place He wanted me to be. I believe another reason God encourages us to look toward heaven is that we may stay focused on the dream and not become distracted with everything around us that seems contrary to the dreams and promises he gives his children.

The night God showed Abraham that vision, Abraham was alone with God. I learned in this valley, no one knows the plans God has for you but you and Him; therefore, like Abraham, I was willing to endure the sacrifice because I knew God would be faithful to what He promised, regardless of how the circumstances looked. I believe this event in Isaac's life allowed him to see how committed his father was to being obedient to God under extreme pressure. He remained faithful, trusting in the promises of God. My children were very observant in my "valley of famine," watching me be obedient to God while God was being faithful to me. Isaac, under extreme pressure in the midst of a famine, moved in obedience and sowed in the land of Gerar, and in that place, he received a hundredfold harvest, meaning he got one hundred times more than what he sowed.

I learned a valuable principle while in my "valley of famine." When things in your life seem like it's no longer growing or producing the desired fruits, continue to sow in that area or place. The land of Gerar is symbolic to an area of life where God simply wants to nurture, even if you think it's not worth the time or investment. The "land of Gerar" could be a marriage, finances, health, family, friends, dreams, goals, prayer life—whatever area or place in your life that's lying dormant. It's not God's intention for us to abandon those places. It's His desire to resurrect it. I've learned it's impossible for me to withdraw anything out of something I haven't sown into or invested in. In my "valley of famine," God wanted to teach me the importance of obedience in the form of sowing. The harder the soil became in my "valley of famine," the more I preached the Word of God. I now preached it with more power and authority than I have ever done before.

The one thing that the valley couldn't touch was my faith and joy for the word of God. *Zara* is the Hebrew word for *sow*.

It means "to be sown upon, to become pregnant, the idea of scattering seed on the ground." In my "valley of famine," there wasn't anything growing around me. Everything seemed to be stagnant. What I didn't realize, there was something growing on the inside of me, which was the word of God. I became impregnated with the Word of God while in the valley, just as Isaac had. Isaac received a hundredfold harvest in the "Land of Gerar" because he gave birth in that land. In my "valley of famine," I learned how to cope with the pressures and stress associated with lack in efforts to ensure I had a healthy pregnancy. God was developing the seed in me while in this "valley," preparing me for something greater, when my wife became pregnant with our first child. I remember the doctor's strict orders of maintaining her stress levels because it could damage or harm the development of the baby, causing still or premature birth. I couldn't allow what was happening all around me to impact in a negative way what was happening on the inside of me. Isaac probably encountered many people trying to convince him to leave Gerar because they couldn't see anything happening in the natural. He faced people who thought he was crazy for believing God can produce a harvest out of dry ground. Everyone is not going to agree with you or understand what God is doing in you while in your "valley of famine," but you have to remember just as I remembered, God didn't place your dream in no one else but you. It's your Dream Live it, your Destiny pursue it, your Life enjoy it. You're the only person who's obligated to see it through until its manifestation. Isaac didn't have to know how God was going to provide the harvest. He only had to believe that God was going to do it. I didn't know how God was going to provide the harvest. I just believed He was going to do it.

The week before our last Sunday at the church, the Lord provided a ram in the bush. The YMCA opened its doors so that we were able to start having service. What a tremendous blessing that was for Psalms Ministries—the first sign that God was at work for us. Amazingly, God would continue to open doors. The last Sunday at the church, after service was over, my family and I went to dinner, and I saw a good friend and true man of God whose church was looking for a senior pastor, and upon hearing my transition immediately, they considered me. They attended several services at the YMCA and were very interested in making me their senior pastor. Opportunities and doors began to open for Psalms Ministries, and a tremendous opportunity became available when I met with my mentor Pastor Grant and his staff at Liberty Baptist, where the hand of God is very evident in that ministry. Potentially, our ministries would partner, and we would become another campus site, which would be a dream come true for me, but what was ironic about this opportunity was we had started communicating about partnering up with Liberty and Pastor Grant about seven years ago, when we first moved into the location we left, but nothing ever materialized, but once the door closed to our old church, it seemed God's timing would be providential.

Although in "the valley of famine" some things dried up such as friendships, finances, and even losing the building, but God spoke to me. He said, "This is the year of restoration. Everything you lost in the famine I will restore and then some." He led me to Deuteronomy 15, where he explains the "the law of the Lord's release." Every seventh year, God releases blessings and liberates the people of God, and 2017 is the year of the Lord's Release. I expect God to do great things for us this year. The valley of famine wasn't designed to defeat me; it was intended for me to gain an appreciation for what I already had and to prepare me for the abundant blessings that are on the way. Isaac knew and I learned in my "valley of famine" not to speak negatively or say anything unless my thoughts were aligned with my destiny. What you think determines what you say, and what you say shapes your reality; therefore, Isaac spoke increase and prosperity while in the midst of stagnation and uncertainty, which produced his harvest in land of Gerar.

In the "valley of famine," your Gerar, you have to speak what you desire to have. Don't wait for the blessing; it's already in you. Give birth to it right where you are. In your valley of famine you may shed a few tears, but just remember Isaac's name means "laughter," and God will have the last laugh once He gives you "victory over the famine."

VULTURES IN THE VALLEY

Vultures in the valley was by far the most problematic valley I endured of my entire valley experience. I had to remind myself and decree every day that "valleys are not designed to defeat me. They are temporary holding places preparing me for the mountain." God reminded me of this fact: "Champions aren't produced on the mountaintops of life. They are celebrated there, and victors, not victims, are made in the valley." In this valley, if you're not careful, you will begin to condemn and beat yourself up, take on the role of a victim seeking justice, vengeance, or much worse, developing a cold heart. In this valley, although I was fronted with my greatest challenges, it magnified the greatest quality I owned. I discovered in this valley that my love for people and my willingness to forgive under every condition now had a bull's-eye on it.

Satan's biggest threat to his kingdom and plans is a "Christ like love," and he will release an onslaught of assaults on whoever is committed to walk in that level of love. In this valley, your destiny is at stake. You may seem as small as David while facing the giant Goliath. It doesn't matter how great the opposition may be, it doesn't matter how large the obstacle or problem seems; you have already been equipped to face your giants in this valley.

David possessed a slingshot, some stones, and a desire to fight for the cause. When you understand that your cause

(God's intended purposes for you) has been challenged, know that your destiny is calling you out. Goliath took one look at David and counted him out. In this valley, people will count you out as if your name is Ichabod (meaning "the Glory of God has departed from you"). *Doxa* is the Greek word for *glory*, which means "splendor, magnificent, favor, from the idea of being very apparent or heavy, weighted down." David understood he was heavily weighted down with the favor of God as he faced Goliath. It is very important in this valley not to be consumed with how people feel or think about you. Joel Osteen said it best: "Everyone has the right to have their own opinion but you have the right to ignore it." Pastor John Hagee said, "Only two people control your destiny, you and God."

David knew he had the favor of God on his side when Goliath proceeded to send curses and insults his way. David heard the "Voice of Destiny" calling out to him. Destiny shouted with Goliath's voice, "Come to me," which empowered David to run straight toward Goliath, shouting toward Goliath but responding to Destiny with actions. "I'm not coming by myself. I come in the name of the Lord of hosts, the God of the armies of Israel who you defied." David killed Goliath in the valley.

In this valley, don't allow fear to keep you from moving closer to your destiny because of the magnitude of problems or circumstances; magnify God bigger than the circumstance. Goliath was bigger than David, but Goliath wasn't bigger than David's God. In this valley you may entertain the thought of running or giving up, but remember, you're building a legacy, and this is a defining moment. Run toward your Goliaths with what's in your hands. God has already equipped you for the battle. David said it best: "Is not there a cause?" The principle is this: "God brought you to it only to bring you through it."

In the book of Esther, Esther, being the main character who is an orphaned Jewish woman raised by her cousin Mordecai, found favor in the king's eye and became queen of Persia. Sometimes in life, we may not understand how and why we arrive at a certain place, and when you can't find the answer, think of a turtle on the fence post. If you ever come across a turtle on the fence, just understand he doesn't possess the strength to get there; therefore, somebody had to put him there. Esther was placed in the Persian Empire as their queen because God knew the Jewish people would one day face genocide, and He needed someone there to intercede. Esther found herself in a "valley of indecision." She knew her life would be at risk if she spoke up on behalf of her people by facing the King without being summoned, but she also knew if she didn't face the King, her people would face genocide. Queen Esther understood there was a cause, and maybe she was brought to the Kingdom of Persia for such a time as this. Giving life to one of my favorite scriptures in the Bible, the queen said, "If I perish, I perish, but I am going to see the king." She knew there was a cause, and she was willing to risk her own life for the cause.

Jesus knew the magnitude of the cause, and He gave His life. God asked me in this valley, "Do you understand the magnitude of your cause, and are you willing to give your life by denying your flesh?" Vultures have a deserved reputation as scavengers, but they have other defining characteristics that are just as distinct. These birds of prey come in a variety of species that share common physical and behavioral characteristics, which make them easily recognizable on all five continents on which they live. I was studying the book of 1 Kings 20 when the title of this chapter was revealed to me. It's a story of King Benhadad (the king of Syria) and thirty-two allied nations planning to besiege King Ahab of Samaria and the people of God. He sent a message to King Ahab threatening him, saying he was going to take all of King Ahab's silver, gold, wives, and children. King Ahab responded and said, "Everything I have is yours." But that wasn't enough for King Ben-hadad; he now demanded to search out the palace of King Ahab and take whatever his men liked. King Ahab summoned some of his advisors and explained to them everything King Ben-hadad was trying to do. They advised him only to give him what he said he would and nothing more. This infuriated King Ben-hadad, and he told his men to prepare to attack, but God had a plan of his own. A prophet came to King Ahab and told him that God was going to deliver into his hands the great army that King Ben-hadad formed. God is faithful to his word and indeed delivered and defeated King Ben-hadad's army. After the defeat, King Ben-hadad's servants had time to assess the battle, and they determined the reason they were defeated was because the battle was fought on the mountain. They believed as long as they fought on the mountain, they would lose the battle because the God of Israel was the God of the mountain and would provide victory for the children of Israel. The servant of King Ben-hadad advised him to wage war against them again the following year, but this time to fight them in the valley. Once again while the enemies of the people of God were strategizing, God sent a prophet to King Ahab again, and the prophet spoke, "Because the Syrians have said, the Lord is God of the mountains and not the Valley's." therefore I will deliver them into your hand again, and you will know that I am the Lord." A wonderful principle began to emerge. Vultures (Scavengers) only pick at the flesh of prey they deem left dead and abandoned. The servants of King Ben-handed concluded that King Ahab and the people of God had been abandoned left for dead by God in the valley.

As this story unfolds, symbolically, King-Ben-hadad and his army represent the vultures in my valley. I observe the many stratagems and reasons they feel confident of dismantling King Ahab and the people of God, who represent the prey. Vultures are not privy to God's omnipresence, meaning He is everywhere. It's imperative to understand God is with you in the valley. Not only is He with you, He is the God of the valley in complete control of everything happening in the valley. David said in the Psalms, "Where can I go from thy spirit, or where can I flee from your presence, if I ascend into heaven you are there if I sleep in hell you are there?" In other words, believers must understand the presence of God is always with us. In this valley, vultures will pick at your flesh relentlessly in attempts to steal your joy, kill your hopes, and destroy your destiny by trying to convince you that God isn't with you.

Scriptures say the joy of the Lord is your strength; the design of a vulture is to exasperate your joy to render you weak and vulnerable. In this valley, you have to be assured of the purposes of Jesus. He came to give us life more abundantly. *Zoe* is a Greek word that means "living life to its absolute fullest, a life only achieved in Jesus Christ." *Perissos* is Greek for *more abundantly*, which means "super abundantly, very highly, beyond measure." God has an extraordinary plan for your life in this valley. You have to be conscious of that truth: therefore when your life seems completely opposite of God's promises, you won't compromise or give up in the valley.

I studied the book of Job when God gave me Job as an illustration for this portion of the chapter. Job was a man who had it all. He loved God, walked in integrity, his character was impeccable, he was a very wealthy and influential man. There came a day when Satan wanted to test Job. He explained to God the only reason Job was serving God in the manner he did was because God had blessed him materially, financially, and God was protecting him and all his assets. In this testing, Job lost everything he had, including the death of all his children; he was afflicted with poor health; and to make matters worse, his wife had given up on God and encouraged him to do the same. This type of suffering most people today cannot relate to. The vultures began to show up in Job's valley, in my opinion, in the form of his friends. His friends heard about everything transpiring in Job's life, and with genuine concern, they come to see about Job, and for seven days they sit quietly, not saying anything to one another. After sitting in silence for seven days, Job finally said something to his friends, which probably shocked them, coming from a God-fearing man, which Job was. He cursed the day he was born.

I tried to put myself in Job's shoes, but it was extremely difficult because of how great he suffered I feel honored to have suffered through, in my opinion, the most difficult time of my life, but in comparison to Job, it was really nothing. Job loved and trusted his friends. He felt comfortable sharing his true feelings with them because they proved themselves to be trustworthy, but what happened next I believe devastated him. The Bible says because Job's friends could not find any answer or reasons why Job was suffering in the manner he was, they began to condemn (express complete disapproval of, typically in public, to criticize, denounce, blame, and berate) him. The actions of his friends is the perfect example of how vultures maneuver in the valley. Job in his vulnerability shared his true feelings with his friends, and instead of comforting him, they began to pick at his flesh.

In this valley, I became vulnerable, sharing my heart with people I believed had my best interest but turned out to be vultures disguised as eagles who soared with me when the wind was blowing beneath my wings, but as soon as I hit some turbulence and forced to land in the valley, they began to unmask themselves. In this valley my sufferings were great a mixture of uncertainty, hurt, and anger. God said, "He was building a greater dependency on Him in me." I couldn't imagine how some of the relationships I built over the years and viewed as undissolvable had all but evaporated. In this valley, vultures picked at my flesh by attacking my character, integrity, and family. The assaults were relentless. I can now relate to why Job became angry. Persecution has no boundaries. The moment I made up in my mind to defend my family's honor, the Lord spoke to me Psalm 59:9: "Because of his strength will I wait upon thee: for God is my defense." God told me "to wait on him. He would defend me, for me to remain in peace." I began to praise God. Vultures in this valley were trying to trick me out of living this abundant life I am called to by picking at the flesh of wounds I received in this valley, picking at the flesh of a wound that hasn't fully healed. First of all, it hurts; it becomes irritated; and if not properly treated, it can become infected. I endured a great deal of hurt and irritation, but what I didn't allow was my heart to become infected, bitter, or cold. I medicated my wounds with the "Word of God." I learned my vultures were spirits, and the only reason I was immersed in a spiritual warfare was because I am a threat to Satan's plans. Scripture says, "Blessed are ye, when men shall revile you, and persecute you, and shall say all manner of evil against you falsely, for my sake." I know that my family is blessed (happy, fortunate, enviable) because we are devoted to the Kingdom of God and fulfilling the plans He has for us. Any amount of success on any level will be met with some form of opposition. The greater the opposition, the greater the opportunity to magnify Jesus Christ.

This valley magnified the greatest quality in me, which is not the ability to teach the Word. My greatest quality that was targeted is my ability to love people unconditionally. You never understand the depths of your love until your love has been opposed at times but not always through various difficult and hurtful situations. The layers of your love begin to be peeled back and revealed to you.

Jesus knew Judas was there to betray him, but the only thing Jesus ever showed Judas was the fact that he loved him. It's important to love people without even questioning their motives. Jesus knew the motives of Judas and still chose to love him. Love is a decision you control who you and how you love. Just let your love be unconditional. My love was thrown in the fire, and it came out pure as gold. My love had to be refined to take out all the impurities, preparing me for my next level and opposition. You can't move on to the next level until you pass the test that's before you.

My sister Shakima Nesbitt told me one day, she said, "Domeka, the last form of love is forgiveness. How can we be believers and not extend forgiveness even to people we know are not sorry for what they've done? They deserve your forgiveness. It's an attribute of love."

Jesus said, "A new commandment I give unto you, as I have loved you, that you also love one another, by this shall all men know that you are my disciples, if ye have love one to another." When you love people, there is an awakening that takes place in other people; people will recognize that you are a disciple, *mathetes* in the Greek, which means "learner, pupil, student, a disciplined follower of Christ," and you become a conduit of His love. The world will know Jesus is with you not so much by what you say but how you live.

Vultures have another distinct quality, and I only can speak for myself in this aspect. I always viewed vultures as scavengers feeding on dead carcasses, but I didn't know how valuable vultures are until I observed them through the eyes of love. Vultures play a valuable role in the ecosystem by disposing of animal waste that would otherwise rot and spread disease. Spiritually, I looked at this fact in a number of ways. We all share some of the same attributes as vultures at one point or another in our lives. Vultures are purposeful; they rid us of the poisons and toxins that could be harmful to someone else. Even the vultures that pick at your flesh while you're in this valley at your lowest, if you're looking at them through the eyes of love, you can still see the good that is within them.

My "valley of vultures" became my "valley of love" and my "valley of purpose." The level of opposition you endure in this valley will lead you to a greater understanding of the depth of your purpose. You become aware of your worth in this valley. You are important to the Kingdom of God more than you realize. The enemy wouldn't attack you with so much velocity if you were just a pawn. Understand, you are Satan's worst nightmare. He's upset with your consistency and commitment to building the Kingdom of God and your unwillingness to quit in the face of difficulty and adversity.

I took notice of how Jesus was opposed in Luke 15:1–2, and how he handled it would set the foundation for me in dealing with my own opposition. The Pharisees and Scribes who were the religious leaders of Jesus's day were considered the upper class of society, very influential and with great authority. They understood scripture but followed their own tradition and legalistic views. Jesus called them hypocrites, saying on the outside they were clean, but in the inside they were full of wickedness (Luke 11:39). The Pharisees and Scribes complained and criticized Jesus because of his willingness to embrace publicans and sinners who were disgraced (meaning "loss of reputation or respect, especially as the result of a dishonorable action"). A publican was a tax collector who worked for the Roman government that oppressed the Jewish people and, in many instances, extorted them out of their money. The publicans were viewed as traitors and outcasts along with other people who had immoral professions, such as harlots (prostitutes). They were rejected by society and the Pharisees and Scribes who questioned and criticized Jesus in Luke 15:2 for eating and spending time with them. Jesus answered their criticism by teaching them three parables or stories of the "Lost Sheep," "Lost Coin," and the "Prodigal Son," which were intended to teach them spiritual and moral truth. All three parables illustrated restoration, redemption, forgiveness, joy, faith, and love, showing His passion and great concern for those who were lost, seeking after them until he found them.

I was very impressed with Jesus's ability to stay committed and focused on His purpose while faced with such extreme criticism. Lebron James, the world's greatest basketball player in my opinion, said, "I like criticism, it makes you strong." He allowed criticism to strengthen him, propelling him to win multiple NBA championships and Most Valuable Player awards. Purpose is defined as the reason for which something is done or created. John F. Kennedy said, "Efforts and courage are not enough without purpose and direction." In other words, know the course or direction of your life; without purpose and direction, it's like releasing arrows from a bow without first identifying the bull's-eye, wasting time and energy which is too valuable.

Jesus knew His purpose! One day while studying in Luke 19 the story of Jesus and Zacchaeus, I discovered another champion like Lebron James in a shorter version, which is Zacchaeus, who just so happens to be a chief publican or tax collector. I was studying the topic of "purpose." While praying, the Lord placed in my spirit a question after first making a decree. He said to me, "You have purpose, but does purpose have you?" He showed me how Jesus as well as Zacchaeus were arrested by purpose. Zacchaeus wanted to see who Jesus was. I believe the publicans in Luke 15 who Jesus ate and spent time with were the employees of Zacchaeus, and they told Zacchaeus all about Jesus and how he loved and embraced them when the other religious leaders rejected and looked down on them.

Jesus one day entered Jericho, and Zacchaeus heard the commotion and excitement at the coming of Jesus because Jesus was very popular in his days, and the crowd surrounding Jesus was so tremendous that Zacchaeus wasn't able to see Jesus through the crowd because of the amount of people and his stature. Zacchaeus was a short man. Zacchaeus, being purpose driven, decided to run and climb up onto a sycamore tree to get a glimpse of Jesus as he passed by, but to his amazement, when Jesus got close to him, Jesus looked up at him and said, "Zacchaeus, come down from that tree quickly because today I must come and abide at your house."

I noticed some things in this encounter, which became paramount to my faith. I noticed how "purpose had Zacchaeus" and spearheaded him into his destiny. Zacchaeus's purpose wouldn't allow his stature or size to become a reason for him to quit or give up. Thomas Edison said, "Our greatest weakness lies in giving up, the most certain way to succeed is always to try just one more time." I refer to Zacchaeus as a champion like Lebron James because a test of a true champion is not whether they can triumph, but whether they can overcome obstacles. An obstacle was before Zacchaeus, and because purpose had him, purpose was able to provide provision for him in the form of a sycamore tree, which elevated him to his destiny. Notice how the sycamore tree in this story was right in the line of Zacchaeus's journey. I learned in my "valley of purpose," when you don't allow your weakness to make you weak, God will provide sycamore trees all around you, elevating you to where God wants you. Look for your sycamore trees while in the valley.

I noticed how Jesus told Zacchaeus that he must come to his house and visit with him. It wasn't even optional for Jesus at this point, and I now understand why. It was because it was connected to Zacchaeus's purpose. Zacchaeus set out to see Jesus. *Eido* is the Greek word for "see," which means "to visit, to have an interview, to be a guest with or to." Zacchaeus climbed that tree with the full intention on meeting Jesus some way and somehow getting his attention to invite him to his house to interview and get to know exactly who he was. Zacchaeus's purpose dictated the course of Jesus's direction that day. Zacchaeus and his family received Jesus Christ into their home and in their hearts, fulfilling the purpose of Jesus Christ, which he stated to Zacchaeus, "For the Son of Man is come to seek and to save that which was lost."

I learned in my "valley of purpose" to live by "stated purposes." It serves as a safeguard against criticism and distractions. I became a champion in the "valley of vultures." Champions are not produced on the mountain; they are celebrated there. Victors, not victims, are produced in the valley.

VALLEY OF FRIENDS

This valley is filled with love, support, comfort, encouragement, and assurance. The "valley of vultures" is a grueling valley charred by loneliness, shame, abandonment, rejection, and indecision. This chapter is inspired by the book of Romans 16, where Paul writes greetings and salutations to as many people he could think who were instrumental to his ministry. He mentioned one couple, Aquilla and Priscilla, who he said put their own lives on the line for the sake of his and the "Kingdom of God." I thought these people were admirable, and I believe God felt it honorable to include them in the canon of scripture. What a tremendous blessing to be included in the Word of God for assisting someone in fulfilling their purposes.

I remember during this valley, a gospel artist and director, Nehemiah Jones, asked me if he could shoot a video at our church, and I said sure. The day of filming, about two hours before the video was to be shot, he asked me if I could play the role of a pastor. I said easy enough; that shouldn't require any acting on my part because it's who I am. While filming, I took notice of when he said, "Action," everything began to move—people on set, objects around the set began to move, things I thought were stationary became alive. I was amazed and very proud of him as well. You never know how talented a person really is until you are invited into their world. He became another person under the anointing of God.

Needless to say, I was very impressed that one moment was a turning point in my life. I took notice of what God was teaching me in that moment. God spoke and said, "The reason you were so astonished was because as you observed him, you were watching Me. Nothing transpires or moves in your life until I say ACTION." Tears instantly began to stream down my face. It was further assurance God was with me and in control of my life. He further said, "When you observe a film or movie for the first time, you aren't aware of how it plays out. You are just a part of the audience enjoying the show, and most people choose to attend a show based on the plot and the cast of actors who are starring in the roles." When the film hits record-breaking numbers or the video goes viral on social media, the director is accredited for his genius, and the actors' stardom further grows until they become larger-than-life figures, box office sensations, $20-million-a-movie earners. The people behind the scenes go unnoticed—the camera crews, makeup artist, stunt doubles. These are the people who don't need a pat on the back, names on billboards, or the celebrity status, content with fulfilling their purposes, understanding without them, there wouldn't be any success.

In the Gospel of John where Jesus fed the multitude of thousands with only five loaves of bread and two small fish they obtained from a little boy, the miracle of multiplication was phenomenal. There is no doubt in my mind Jesus could have summoned bread out of the air and fish out of the sea, but I believe he wanted us all to understand the principle of the background people. Without the little boy and his food, there wouldn't have been any miracle performed that day, but in scripture, I tend to read over that verse, but now God is placing emphasis on the background people who serve as pillars to success. When I speak of success in reference to my valley experience, I speak in regards of people who contributed to the peace, joy, comfort, hope, and encouragement I gained while in the "valley of vultures." God has blessed me with a tremendous family. My wife and children have been with me every step of the way, holding my arms up in like manner as Aaron and Hur.

In the day when Moses and Israel fought against Amalek in the Valley of Rephidim, which is called Massah, meaning "test," Moses instructed Joshua to build an army of men prepared for war, and Moses would stand on the "mountain" with the "rod of God" in his hand. Joshua went out to do battle, and Moses stood on the mountain with his arms raised, and as long as his arms were raised, Joshua and the children of Israel prevailed, but when Moses let his arms down, Amalek would prevail. Moses's hands and arms became tired, so a stone was placed under him so he could sit down. While he was sitting, Aaron and Hur stood on each side of him, raising his arms until the sun began to set. Joshua and Israel defeated Amalek and his armies. God instructed Moses to write down the events so it could be included in scripture. Moses constructed an altar and named it Jehovah-Nissi (the Lord is my Banner).

Ancient armies carried standards or banners that served as marks of identification and as symbols that embodied the ideals of a people. Like a flag, a banner was something that could be seen from afar, serving as a rallying point for troops before a battle. The Lord is our Jehovah-Nissi, and I thank God for my wife and children carrying those standards and identifying themselves with Jesus Christ. They rallied together with me in the valley and placed a stone under me when I became weary of fighting this spiritual battle. They recognized that as long as my arms were raised up to Jesus Christ, then we would continue to prevail.

In the valley I got extremely tired, physically and mentally, becoming stressed out, frustrated, irritated, angry, feeling abandoned by God, thinking that he wasn't sympathetic to my situation, rejected by people. In those moments, my arms would get weary, and my family could sense the hurt. In those moments, they would lift up my arms like Aaron and Hur, restoring me to a place where I could continue to fight. My wife would encourage me greatly with scripture and reassure me of the fact that God called me, and He would always be with me. I would quickly repent to the Lord, and just seeing the joy and hope in the eyes of my children made it all worth fighting for.

One day while having family time, we watched a movie called *Ben Hur*, and while we were watching the movie, God spoke to me, and I shared with my family who Hur was in the Bible. I will not give full details of the movie because I don't want to spoil it for those of you who haven't seen it, but I highly recommend it. The movie was so powerful, my family and I wanted to watch it a second time because of the message and principles that it taught, but what I didn't realize at the time God was revealing to me exactly what my family was enduring and the price they were paying for holding my arms up like Aaron and Hur held up Moses. The movie brought tears to my eyes, and at that moment, I gained a great appreciation for my wife and my children. God revealed to me the depths of their love for their husband and father. My family are my background people and my number one "valley friends."

I was reading one of my favorite stories in the Bible in 2 Chronicles 20, and it's a story of King Jehoshaphat of Judah, and he endured a battle in the valley against the children of Moab and Ammon, the Moabites and Ammonites, which are distant relatives of Judah. When the battle was over, scriptures say the people assembled themselves together in the valley.

God spoke to me instantly, and the phrase and chapter "Valley Friends" was born. A "valley friend" is a person who God brings into your life while you are in the midst of fighting for your life; oftentimes the "valley friend" isn't even aware that you are going through anything, especially something as difficult as the lowest place in your life. Valley friends are not chosen by you; they are chosen by God. Valley friends are the least likely people you would ever think who would be a source of hope or encouragement for you. Some of my "valley friends" are people I thought didn't even like me, and also I discovered later many of my "valley friends" were enduring their own valley experiences the same time I was enduring mine. "Valley friends" emerge while the vultures are preoccupied with feasting on your flesh.

God taught me a powerful principle, which I will share after I mention some of my notable "valley friends."

Steve and Karen Barrs are the epitome of Proverbs 18:24: "Friends that stick closer than a brother." I can write a novel about this couple, about their unwavering support and love that they have shown over the years to my family not just in the valley but even on the mountaintops of life. Their friendship has been consistent and honorable. Steve refers to me as an energy giver, and Karen is the most down-to-earth person I know. Without them I wouldn't have made it out of the valley.

Pastor Keion Henderson, senior pastor of the Lighthouse Church of Houston, inspired me greatly. Watching his ministry from afar, applying some of the truths and practical principles and quotes such as "To go from poor to powerful, you must *stop giving* permanent passes to people who were only supposed to have a day pass to your life." I learned through his teachings, it's okay to move on from people who you thought you couldn't go on without.

Joel Osteen, the senior pastor of Lakewood Church in Houston, through his ministry, teachings of hope, and quotes such as "Everyone has the right to have their own opinion about you, and you also have the right to ignore it." I learned tremendously from his ministry. I relate very much so with Pastor Joel Osteen from the standpoint of our personalities; we want everyone to like us as if everyone is supposed to be our friend. I learned through his teachings that it's okay to want people to like you, but not at the expense of trying to win them over. It's best to invest your time in relationships with people who celebrate you as opposed to those who criticize you. I am also encouraged greatly by Pastor Joel Osteen's willingness to stay focused on his purpose and destiny despite all the attacks against his character, integrity, and ministry. I listen to his radio broadcast, and he taught a practical principle on how to stay focused while under attack. He said that he doesn't listen to or read any of the negative comments or stories. In other words, he doesn't allow it to penetrate his spirit. The principle is don't entertain negativity about you nor someone else, don't lend your ear to it.

Pastor Anthony Williams, who serves as Paul to me as I am Timothy to him, writes letters of encouragement to me as often as he can, stirring up the gift that's inside of me, without any expectation of me writing him back. I love that man of God.

Words cannot ever begin to suffice for the gratitude I have for Pastor and First Lady Watkins. They both have a heart and ear for God, always lifting my family up in prayer and seeing the best in us. Pastor Watkins consistently reminds me to "trust God all the way."

My cousin Elder Fletcher, a powerful woman of God and my favorite preacher, spoke greatness over my life, reminding me that God had infused greatness in me and that I had the tools to accomplish anything I set out to do. She told me to shoot for my dreams, become an author, professor, basketball coach, and not to settle for mediocrity, but to use what was in my hand.

My closest cousin, Olasaun "Peanut" Parker. We grew up like brother and sister. We are the same age, even though she acts and thinks she's my mother. She always protected me, an angel God sent me. I am so proud of her and all her accomplishments. Her success doesn't surprise me. I always knew she would be great; she's very distinguished.

Deacon Todd and Candice Wharton with my goddaughter Jess, Pastor Grant and Ms. Tammy, Pastor Norton and First Lady Norton, Kenny Harrell, Ethel Martin, Gloria Lassiter, Tiara Darden, Kenya Chester, Laticia Daugett, Arethea Walker, Naomi and Nia, "Mother Neal" (the mother of our church), and Darlene George, who serve as great pillars in my life. Their unconditional love for my family is heart melting.

Carlton and Belinda Watkins along with my godsons Tyson, Tyler, and Carlton Jr.; Kimberly Williams and my goddaughter Danni; Earthlum and Shan Williams. My parents, Mr. and Mrs. Grafton Marshall, always kept me laughing when we would hang out together. They reminded me to always enjoy life and don't allow anything to steal my joy. My sister and best friend, April Lucy-bell Kelley. Her belief in me is so strong that she made me think I could overcome every obstacle that stood in the way of my destiny. Shontae Harris, my sister-in-law, who stood firm and faithfully by my wife's side, seeing the greatness in us and the need for unwavering support and guidance, stepped into my life with the foot of God and said, "I got you, big bro. Let's move forward in the Spirit of Excellence."

Deacon Willie "String Bean" Mack, Deacon James Chester, Pastor Lennon Wynn, Deacon Rufus "Bear" Jones and Kim "PK" Jones, Deacon Dominique and Ahnjala George, Deacon Biggs and Minister Biggs, Shania Jones, Al Maven, Pierre Russell, Randy and Shakima Nesbitt, Amir Nesbitt, Jayce "Dink" Moore, Uncle Chico and Aunt Terry.

Dwayne Thomas, one day him and I were at work having a conversation in the basement right in front of the morgue. He was telling me about a situation he had with I believe one of his basketball players, which happens to be a young lady. She was telling him how much she appreciated him and thanked him for always showing her unconditional love and support. She began to talk about all these great qualities that a true father possesses, and he responded to her, "Wow, you have a great dad," and she replied, "I was talking about you." Dwayne, at this point in our conversation, he began to cry, and he thanked the young lady for seeing him in that light as an example of how a father should be. Then he encouraged me. He said, "I look at you as my pastor, friend, and brother. I know what you've been going through these past few years, and I never mentioned any of it to you, but what I learned from you is that you never give up, and it doesn't matter how difficult a situation is. You keep loving people, and you always came to work with a smile on your face." He explained to me just like the young lady explained to him all the qualities that a follower of Jesus should have, and he said, "When I think of Jesus, I think of you." I began to cry like a baby. Those were the most encouraging words I ever received in my life. My only desire is that people see the qualities of Jesus Christ in me, and every believer should feel the same way. I'm not perfect, but Jesus isn't looking for perfection; he's looking for persistence.

Anthony Deloatch, Phillip "Dr. Phil" Jenkins, Walter "Walt" Phillips, James Andrews, John and Kim Harris, Cliff and Eva Stokes, Kevin Harris, Robert Bland, Devon Kelley, Ezra Gant, Demetrius "Duke" Phipps, Tim Williams, Mr. and Mrs. Shameek Baker, Ananias Moss Jr., Tim Williams, Ron Moore, Demetrius Rush, Mr. and Mrs. Daniel Nice, Wajheeda Shaw, Jamando and Asia Towler, the entire Psalms Ministries Church Family, coworkers Budd Proctor (boss), Russ, Tom, Mark, Ron, Shorty, Mr. Ken, Carol and Mike. Ronald Lindsey, founder/CEO of Laughter As Medicine Production (LAMP), whose mission is "changing the world one laugh at a time." I refer to Ronald Lindsey as my "Ananias," meaning "favored of the Lord." Ronald is favored of the Lord. His many spiritual gifting is a testament to who he is in Christ. He is an awesome visionary.

Ananias was sent by the Lord to Saul of Tarsus, who would become known as the Apostle Paul, the great author of 1/3 of the New Testament, to restore his sight after being blinded by the miraculous visitation he had with Jesus Christ. I believe the Lord sent Ronald Lindsey to me to restore my sight, my spiritual vision. He encourage me to enlarge my territory like Jabez, to pick up my rod like Moses, to dream big like Noah. Hope and restoration was infused in me after every conversation I had with him. He calls me *teacher* and said that I possess a unique ability to teach the Word of God and that my ministry would become a church without walls. Simply put, I love him, and without his vision, I wouldn't see clearly who I am today.

Sandra Jones who fed me breakfast at work whenever I was hungry, like the ravens who fed Elijah in 1 Kings 17:6. Melinda Deal, my best friend at work who I see every morning smiling bright like the sun. Robin Wilkins, my praise partner at work;

Mrs. Francis Coleman, whose joy is contagious; and the amazing Mrs. Sharon Alexander, who daily gives me motivation and inspirational stories at work. Team Egeiro, my AAU boys basketball team, Nakia Gouveia, Jakeim Roberson, Kellen Marshall, Darrius Tunnell, Teko Dunlap, Marion Moore, Justice Smith, Juwuan Brown, Steven Sayles, Jordan Boone, Coach Markel, and Coach Naizell Cooper keep a lookout for these guys. They one day will be playing professional basketball.

These are just a few of my "valley friends" who served as a great support team and inspiration during a time I felt as if I had disappointed Jesus. Similar to the emotions I believe Peter experienced when he denied Jesus three times after Jesus had foretold him that he would, in that moment, Jesus looked at Peter, and Peter rehearsed the words of Jesus in his mind: "Before the cock crows, thou shalt deny me thrice." Scripture reads after that moment, Peter walks out and wept full of sorrow and guilt. In my valley, I felt ashamed and guilty, which is a normal emotional response when you're at the lowest place in your life. You tend to blame yourself for everything that has transpired. I wonder if Peter wrestled with the thought of if Christ still loved him or not because that became a recurring thought in my mind. I played it over and over and over again as if it was my favorite song. There was no validity to Peter's thought, but sometimes I allowed those accusing voices to begin to speak negativity and lies to my spirit.

According to Revelations 12:10 Satan is called the accuser of the brethren, who accuse us day and night before God, and I would entertain those thoughts that would allow me to feel condemned and guilty, but scripture clearly teaches in Romans 8:1, "There is therefore now no condemnation to them which are in Christ Jesus, who walk not after the flesh but after the Spirit." Conviction is great, especially when it leads to repentance and not condemnation. We don't have the right or authority to walk around living in guilt or condemnation. What that is saying in essence is that I died for myself, and I have undone everything that Christ has afforded for us in paving the way of salvation by his death. I received my reassurance that Jesus loved me while at my lowest because he showed his love for me and you in dying for you and I while at our lowest (Romans 5:8). I obtained further evidence of Jesus Christ showing love to Peter, even from the very "Throne of Heaven" after ascending back home to the father.

In Acts 3, a very familiar and miraculous event takes place of a man who was crippled from birth and becomes healed by two of Jesus's disciples operating in his "Name." I want to place emphasis on the two disciples who were in a partnership "Koinonia," connected by Christ together to carry out that purpose. Peter, the disciple who is widely known for denying Jesus, and John, the disciple who is widely known to be loved by Jesus. My "valley friends" are more important to me than they realize. When they showed up in my valley, it wasn't just them; they brought the love of Jesus with them. I can imagine how Peter felt when he was able to connect with the Apostle John. He knew that he was still connected to the love of Christ. Through my "valley friends," just them showing up reminded me that I was still connected to the love of Jesus Christ. The principle is this: in your valley, you may feel disconnected from Christ, but he will send you "valley friends" to assure you that you are still connected. Thank you, "valley friends," for your connection, your hookup to Jesus Christ.

VALLEY OF BLESSINGS

 $\mathcal{T}$ he story of King Jehoshaphat as he fought against the Moabite and Ammonite armies presented great truth and principles that I was able to apply to my life while in my "valley experience." It was told to King Jehoshaphat beforehand that the armies that turned out to be a great multitude were preparing to attack them. Jehoshaphat was warned. God has a way of preparing his people for their "valley experience" or battles, and two years prior to my "valley experience," God was preparing me through various sermons I preached and sermons from other pastors I heard.

Through praying and seeking the face of God, we enter every year with a theme. The first year before my "valley experience" was the year of "expansion and elevation." When something is elevated, it rises, becomes vertical. God showed me a vision of a person standing tall south to north. In that same vision with the same theme in mind, he showed me expansion, which means something is expanding or being stretched. He showed me a man standing tall now with his arms stretched out wide east to west. Now observing this man in the vision, the Lord showed me the man was in the shape of a cross. The entire year I kept the cross of Christ before me, remembering his passion and the sacrifices he made for us, but what I didn't realize was two years later, I would have to bear my own cross, suffering tremendous persecution on a level I've never experienced before while in the "valley." The entire year I was preaching and teaching on "expansion and elevation," I was looking for growth numerically, financially, and spiritually. I was waiting to see the harvest of the seeds that were being sown. I was growing spiritually, waiting for something supernatural to take place in the natural realm, but the year ended, and I was still in expectation. Not only did things not grow in the natural, but everything was stagnant.

We entered the next year full of zeal and anticipation as God spoke, "Kingdom Living" as our theme. I was very excited about this series of teaching. God told us we were going "to the Crown to the Cross and back to the Crown." Our focus was on the six kingdom literature books in the Old Testament. The purpose was for us to gain an understanding of the "Kingship of God," which is symbolic of the Crown. God had a plan for the people of God in the Old Testament. He wanted to be their "King," a Theocracy with Him ruling over the people, but they rejected His plan. They wanted to have a king just like the other nations of people with man ruling over them, a monarchy. God explained to them what a kingdom would look like without him serving as king. He literally read them their rights and gave them exactly what they wanted. Then came King Saul. Here comes John the Baptist preaching the good news of the "Kingdom of God" after the *intertestamental period*, which is the Protestant term, and *deuterocanonical period* is the Catholic and Orthodox Christian term for the gap of time between the period covered by the Hebrew Bible and the period covered by the Christian New Testament. Traditionally, it is considered to cover roughly four hundred years, spanning the ministry of Malachi (420 BC) to the appearance of John the Baptist in the early first century AD. It is known by members of the Protestant community as the "400 Silent Years" because it is believed to have been a span where God revealed nothing new to his people. Can you imagine not hearing from God for four hours, let alone four hundred years? John the Baptist is now preaching and saying to the people, "Hey, I got good news, God wants to be your king again, but this time, it's not on a national or geographical basis. It's through obtaining a personal relationship with Jesus Christ." Therefore, Jesus died for us, providing salvation for anyone who will believe and accept him. The Cross serves as a symbol of salvation. *Soteria* is a Greek word for salvation, which means "deliverance, salvation, welfare, prosperity, preservation, safety."

Christians can identify with the Cross readily because of all the benefits that come with salvation. Salvation to believers is eternal life, an endless experience in the presence of God on earth and in heaven, and all the bells and whistles that come with it on the earth such as prosperity, protection, and deliverance. I can identify with a prosperity message, a message of security and hope, which is great, but before the Cross was the Crown and the Lord desire greatly, and it's time for us to go back to the Crown that we may truly appreciate the Cross.

The Cross points to Jesus as the Savior, but the Crown points to Jesus as the King. We accept him as Savior, but hesitant to allow him to sit on the throne of our hearts as King. Accepting the Crown is relinquishing control of your life, becoming the passenger instead of the driver of your life. Your will is now immersed into His will, and you understand your every move is being orchestrated by the guiding symphony of His hands. Matthew 6:33 says, "But seek ye first the Kingdom of God and His righteousness and all these things shall be added unto you." Making Jesus King requires us to put him first in our life, making us completely subjective to him in every area of our life. The entire year I was preaching and teaching the "Kingdom of God," waiting for something supernatural to take place in the natural, but what I didn't realize was a lifestyle God was calling me into, and my valley experience was the vehicle God used to drive me to that destination.

Scripture says after Jehoshaphat defeated their enemies, they gathered in the valley on the fourth day and celebrated. Jehoshaphat and the children of Israel fought in the Valley of Tekoa. They changed the name of that valley into the Valley of Berachah, which means "the Valley of Blessing." The principle is this: God doesn't have to take you out of the valley to bless you. He can bless you in the valley. God can bless you while you are in the lowest places of your life. I was practically begging God to deliver me from the valley when God showed me this truth. God reminded me that this "valley isn't designed to defeat me, it's a temporary holding place preparing me for the mountain." The valley isn't designed to hold you back; it's there to push you forward. Jehoshaphat and the children of Israel celebrated on the fourth day after the victory because they were so overwhelmed with taking away all the spoils of victory the first three days.

Revisit the story of Job again. After he endured his "valley of suffering," scripture says God gave him two times more than he had before, and that his later days were more prosperous than the former. God will give us double for our trouble. The spoil is everything deemed valuable or worth taking after the battle for the victor. Spoil is the prize, and in this case, it was so much that it took them three days to carry it all with them. I remember being in the valley at this point, asking God to show me specific purposes so I could discover exactly what He wanted me to learn and carry away with me as my spoil. I didn't want to miss any opportunity to grow because the valley is riddled with teachable moments. The principle is this: while in the valley, don't allow your spoil or valuables to become a casualty, but hasten to add to the storehouse of your mind by learning and growing.

I took this very important fact with me from this battle. In biblical days, it was customary for the victors, upon winning a battle, to kill all the men, leaving their dead bodies behind so they could gather all the women and children, ensuring the strength of the people was depleted so there wouldn't be any way the people could reorganize and overpower them at some later time. This truth strengthened me and reminded me of the purposes and order of God for a man. I love being married. I think it's the greatest relationship God created, and oftentimes married couples find themselves in "valley experiences," only to become a casualty of the valley ending in divorce. Fifty percent of marriages in the United States dissolve. I view marriage as a ministry, and it's extremely important and foundational for the Christian home, and I believe we as believers possess the truths the world needs to attack this problem. I approach this fact with all sincerity. I believe if the man is taken out of the home, the strength, leadership, and security is taken from that home, forcing mothers and wives to fulfill roles they were never designed to fulfill, and quite honestly, they do a great job, but they shouldn't have to bear that burden. As a man, husband, and father, I understand how valuable I am to the overall well-being and development of my family in the home and society abroad, but most importantly, I understand the plan and order of God.

We have to remember, Satan opposes everything God proposes. In my valley experience, I was awakened by the fact that marriages are under spiritual attack, and we as Christians have to be examples of how God intended for this union to function. Husbands are to love their wives in the manner Jesus Christ loved the church. The church, not the edifice or building, but the "*ekklesia,*" an assembly of Christians who are hoping for eternal salvation through Jesus Christ, a body of believers. Jesus gave his life for the church, and we as husbands should give ours as well for our wives. Statistics show more than 20 million children live in a home without the physical presence of a father, while millions more have dads who are physically present but emotionally absent. I understand the order of God, and so does my wife and children, and as a pastor, I have to be mindful that I am not neglecting my family by positioning the church ahead of them. It's God first, family, and then the church. I'm not so consumed with Church and the demands it places on your life that I am not being the pastor and father of my home first. My children expect me to be at their basketball games, cheerleading functions, school meetings, and family gatherings. I've learned when nobody else is in your corner, your family will be. I owe them the bulk of my time and my undivided attention. Make your family your priority.

My mother, the matriarch of our family, stressed the importance of us having family dinners, mostly after church on Sundays. My wife plans movie night mainly on Tuesdays, teaching our children the importance of spending time with your family. It's the small things in life that mean the most and often leave an impression or pattern that your children will follow when they have their own families. My wife and children, we're like a lion's pride. We stick together. They're my closest friends. If you see one Kelley, the rest of us are somewhere in the vicinity. Dick Woodward would always say to me, "Wherever you are, be there," meaning make sure you are fully invested and engaged. I grew up without a father in my home, and while analyzing this research, I compared the results to certain behavior patterns I possessed, and I concluded the information I obtained was accurate. Growing up without a father could alter the structure of the brain and produce children who are more aggressive and angry. I unequivocally agree. Even while playing basketball as a kid throughout my high school years, I played with anger and aggression, which stemmed from me not having a father in my home. But now that I am a basketball coach, I can identify quickly and relate with a player who's going through what I've been through based on the way he approaches the game of basketball. It's as if every time you step on the basketball court, you're proving your worth to a father who doesn't see your value, hoping that eventually he accepts you. Research also suggests children bought up only by a single mother have a higher risk of developing deviant behavior, including drug abuse, and ultimately engaging in activity that leads to juvenile incarceration and prison stints.

I rebelled greatly against male authority and had little respect for any male figures, which ultimately landed me in juvenile detention. I learned valuable lessons and took a tremendous amount of spoil from my "valley experience" in the form of truth and principle. I was determined not to lose anything in the valley. I discovered God wasn't setting me back; He was setting me up. I maintained my joy while in the valley, my peace stayed intact, and my faith and trust in Jesus grew stronger every day. I entered the valley strong but came out stronger, just like the children of Israel in the book of Exodus. The more they were afflicted, the more they multiplied and grew.

In the book of James, James said, "Dear brothers, is your life full of difficulties and temptations, then be happy, for when the way is rough, your patience has a chance to grow, so let it grow, and don't try to squirm out of your problems, for when your patience is finally in full bloom, then you will be ready for anything, strong in character, full and complete." The valley produces maturity of character, which is a ripe fruit of patience. Character is the mental and moral qualities distinctive to an individual, your personality, nature, disposition, makeup. In the valley I developed patience; prior to the valley I wasn't able to forbear and persevere through difficulties. I would become frustrated to a point where I would think irrationally. I wasn't aware that I possessed the fortitude to withstand as much as I did in the valley. I understand how important character is to the Lord. You can have every spiritual gift and operate in faith that moves mountains, but without character, you're nothing more than a tinkling symbol making noise.

I gained great insight while observing Jehoshaphat in the valley of blessing. He was able to be honest with God when he discovered he was under the threat of attack. Honest like Moses when God spoke to him from out of the burning bush, calling for him to deliver the children of Israel from the bondage of Pharaoh and the Egyptians. Moses said, "Why send me? Send Aaron, my brother. I have a speech impediment. I can't speak on your behalf." God responded, "If I wanted an eloquent speaker, I would have created you eloquent."

Scripture says Jehoshaphat was afraid, and therefore, he prayed to God. The principle is this: it's okay to be honest with God, expressing how we feel. Jehoshaphat admitted he didn't know what to do and was inclined to pray, seeking instruction from God. I was always told growing up when you don't know what to do, always do what you feel is the right thing to do, but now I understand when I am without resolution, I simply must go to God in prayer, admitting my fears and uncertainties. I was afraid while in the valley. Jehoshaphat understood the ramifications of losing a battle, the loss of lives, homes, his reputation, and influence. I battled with the fear of losing everything while in the valley, everything I had obtained by the Grace of God. I didn't know what to do. I had no answers. I humbled myself before God and said, "If you don't intervene, Father, I perish. Don't allow the expectations of my enemies to fall upon me." I believe that honest prayer reached heaven in a matter of seconds because God began to speak to my spirit instantly. As my attention stayed focused on Jehoshaphat and how he maneuvered while in the valley, I came to the verse where God told him, "Be not afraid or dismayed by reason of this great multitude: for the battle is not yours, but God's." I began to praise God and shout in my house like blind Bartimaeus was shouting and calling, "Jesus thou son of David." He shouted and praised Jesus so much, the people tried to quiet him down, but the more they tried to silence him, the louder he became. It was about five on a Sunday morning when God revealed this to me, and I woke up everyone in my house with my shouts of joy unto the Lord. My wife and children thought something was wrong. They all came running down the stairs to check on me, and even the dog was barking loud, trying to enter the house from the garage. He even thought something was wrong. In that moment, the entire burden I was carrying for the past two years had been lifted. I was completely free spiritually.

God further instructed Jehoshaphat. He told he him that he wasn't needed to fight in the battle, but to stand still and see the salvation of the Lord. The duration of this valley, I thought it was my fight. I was fighting as hard as I could with everything I had. Then all of a sudden, God instructed me to take a step back, stand still, and see His deliverance. God immobilized me. I was refrained now from making decisions on my own, following my own lead. I had to abandoned my military strategy; it was time to discard my plans. I've done everything I could, prayed every prayer, made all the necessary moves; now he wanted me to sit back and completely trust His plan. It is amazing how God simply wants us to stand still while faced with any adversity or valley experiences.

Jesus rested while in the stern of the boat while the wind and waves were beating against and filling the boat with water, and finally the disciples awoke him, and he said to the wind, "Peace, be still." The wind ceased, and there was a great calm. Jesus wants his children to be able to rest in the midst of any storm or valley. There is a rest promised to believers who enter into it by faith. Jesus asked his disciples where was their faith and that faith in him provides us with the grace to be able to keep us at peace. Hebrews 4:10 says, "Let us labor therefore to enter into that rest, lest any man fall after the same example of unbelief." The children of Israel are the example of not obtaining that rest because rejecting the Word of God, their disobedience caused them to come short of that rest, which was promised to them. The promise of rest is extended to us by the preaching of the Word of God today, but only received when we hear and receive the word by faith. The principle is this: no matter how difficult or trying the valley is, your rest is available when your faith or trust in Jesus Christ is intact.

Jehoshaphat bowed down and worshipped God as a sign of surrender. His actions were exemplary, so I followed his lead and surrendered as well. Once Jehoshaphat surrendered, he told the people to believe in the Lord, and your hearts will be established, and you will prosper. I began to have complete confidence and trust in the Lord, and He began to prosper me in the valley. God implemented His own plan for Jehoshaphat and for me. God used worship to confuse the enemies of Jehoshaphat. The people of God began to sing praises to the Lord, and God set ambushes for the enemies of Jehoshaphat, and when the people began to sing, their enemies were so confused, they began to kill each other until they all were destroyed.

Praise and worship is the most powerful tool we are equipped with to fight against our enemies. Your adversary won't expect you to praise God when you're down and out at your lowest. It confuses the enemy when you're smiling full of joy instead of being defeated and depressed. I maintained my joy and smile because ultimately, I knew God had a plan for my life. My story would not end in defeat. God expects us to be full of joy and praise him all the way to the "victory line." We just don't praise God for what He does or when everything is going well that's seeking His hand. We should praise him for who He is that's seeking His face. Our praise should be consistent, not predicated on how much or what we have, but praise God in the valley and on the mountain. It was so powerful how Jehoshaphat changed the name of his valley. It was as if he grabbed his destiny by the horns. That was a turning point for me. It gave me insight of how our perspective should be during every valley experience. My victory came the moment my perspective changed, not my circumstances. Oftentimes we wait until the things surrounding our circumstances change. We look for little signs or rays of hope before we believe or reach that turning point when we grab our destiny by the horns. There was no evidence of things getting better before my turning point of perspective changed. Actually, they were indeed getting worse for me prior to the turning point of my perspective change. My circumstances began to shift in a favorable direction moments after my perspective changed, renaming my valley to the Valley of Victory.

Romans 8:28 states, "All things work together for the good of those who love the Lord and are called according to His purposes." Even though the valley at times looked as if it was going in the complete opposite direction of where I believe God was taking me, everything that was transpiring—the good, bad, and ugly—God was using it for His good. Some way, somehow, everything is salvageable to God. No experience is wasted, and at some point, it benefits you because it's necessary for your development in your destiny. God gave me "eagle perspective in the valley." Reading Pastor Dick Woodward's book *As Eagles How to Be an Eagle Disciple*, I learned qualities about eagles that help to shape my outlook. The vision of an eagle is monocular and binocular, meaning they have the ability to see at a great distance, and they can sharply focus their eye to see objects up close. I learned one of the reasons they like to build their nests eight to ten thousand feet above sea level is that with their extremely acute vision, they can see prey in valley thousands of feet below. From their nest, they can see a rabbit or some other small animal that we humans could not see when the animal is thousands of feet below. When you break the word *perspective* down, the word literally means "to look through" (per = through, specto = look). The expression "tunnel vision" is a good paraphrase of the word *perspective*. The person with tunnel vision sees their objective as if through a tunnel, and they are oblivious to all the obstacles and distractions that could keep them from accomplishing their goals or objectives.

While in the midst of the valley, I was now able to see through or past the ground level of the valley. I was able to soar like an eagle, rising above every circumstance in the valley. I developed a tunnel vision on my destiny, and before I knew it, I was soaring at altitudes in my life I never reached before, understanding I was like an eagle seated in heavenly places. My mentor, Pastor Woodward, teaches an awesome principle in reference to an eagle's perspective. He said, "Jesus showed us the importance of our perspective when He told us our lives can be filled with happiness or with sadness, and those two opposites are determined by what Jesus calls our 'eye.'" Jesus was referring to how we see things. According to Jesus, if the way you see things is healthy or whole, your life will be filled with joy or light. If your eye—meaning your outlook, your mindset, or your perspective—is not healthy but defective, your life will be filled with darkness, meaning unhappiness, sadness, and depression. My perspective changed; therefore, my outlook was completely different than it was when I entered the valley. I had to make some difficult adjustments in my life. If I was determined to be an eagle, then I had to surround myself with eagles; my "surround sound" had to change, meaning the people that were in my circle of trust and friends. I believe if you're the person everyone leans on in the group, I wouldn't recommend you leave that circle because the people there need you, but I do suggest you get an adjacent circle where you can grow, which consists of people you can learn from and lean on.

I now have what I call the "eagle's nest," people who are already extremely successful in areas of life where I know God is leading me to according to my gifts and talents. It's important to know your gifts and talents or skill set because they point you in the direction where God is leading. My eagle's nest consists of Steve Barrs and Kevin Harris, two very intelligent God-fearing businessmen who I admire and lean on for business advice and support. Steve Barrs not only serves as a mentor in that area; he just so happens to be one of my very best friends, my brother, and my counselor at times with an awesome prayer life, which is exemplary. His sound advice has challenged me at times to really look within and seek out everything God has for me. Steve doesn't mind having the hard conversations with me, tell-it-like-it-is conversations. I appreciate that very much.

Kevin Harris quickly climbed the ladder of my friends with his unwavering support of my family and AAU basketball organization. He is an advocate for Jesus, willing to give of his time and talents to further someone's vision. Pastor Grant, my mentor who is the leading pastor of one of the fastest growing ministries in the Virginia area. Demetrius "Coach Duke" Phipps, in my opinion, is the greatest high school basketball coach I've been around, and now I have the opportunity to work with and learn from, and he is one of the most genuine people you would ever know. He's like a brother to me. Attorney Carl C. La Mondue, a prominent lawyer and friend of over fifteen years, who has maintained Godly character and helped me to see God in some of my most darkest moments. His positive influence, counsel, and determination gave me hope to reach for stars and become everything God has intended me to be. Alvin Maven, a very successful businessman, father figure to me, godfather to my son, the most optimistic and well-rounded person I know, he can have a conversation with anybody. He taught me life and the ways of the world. I was only eighteen years of age when he came into my life and began to teach me the true responsibilities of a man. I was young and unwilling to trust anyone at the time, but he came in and quickly gained my trust and respect. Still to this day, whenever I speak to him, which is often, I refer to him as Pops. He is a great business mind who showed me practical things about business that actually became life lessons to me.

I remember one of the first things he taught me was the importance of relationships. I remember going with him to the bank on several different occasions, but he would always go to the same bank teller's line; he wouldn't allow anyone else to serve him. He would go to the same bank at the same time on the same day, and finally, I asked him why, and it got kind of deep then. He said, "The reason I go to the same person every time is because you never burn bridges in life because you never know when or if you might need that person ever again." So the next time we went to the bank, I believe he purposely left his wallet in the car and was able to complete his bank transaction without an ID, simply because he had built a relationship with the bank teller. I was amazed, but that's how he has been teaching me for the past twenty years, and I apply every lesson. So when God sends someone into your life, you honor them and cherish the relationship.

Phillip Jenkins, my friend and business partner who just may be the greatest father and barber I've seen. I admire his perspective on life and his desire to serve as a pillar in the community. He prayed for me the entire time I was in the valley. I know God has great plans for us; he's my brother. Todd Wharton "Deacon Todd" is a true man of God who is faithful, loyal, and always had my back. I thank God for him. We were saved together. God called us into ministry together, and he is the epitome of how a true friend should be. The best is yet to come for us, Deacon Todd. Thank you for never giving up on me. Your humility is a true sign of the strength and courage you possess. You are the greatest armor bearer any pastor could have. It's an honor to stand by your side.

Pastor Dick Woodward is the most prolific Bible teacher I've ever encountered. Although he is in heaven, he left me with enough material, which should last me a lifetime. Shontae Harris, my sister and the administrator of our ministry, is phenomenal; her resilience and dedication to leading with a spirit of excellence is remarkable. Her level of professionalism is the benchmark, and her desire to please God in everything she does is exemplary. I rest secure knowing that our ministry and businesses are secure in her hands. Her unwavering support for me in my valley was astronomical.

Each of these great men and women of God are excelling in an area God has called me to and are more than willing to serve as mentors to me in some great capacity. I understand although I may not be at the top of my "eagle's nest" because my wife is at the top of this eagle's nest with a close eye on all of us. When I think about my entire valley experience, my appreciation and adoration for my wife has become deeper, and her voice is the most prominent voice in my life outside of God, of course. I never undervalued my wife. She has always been the shine in my brightest day, but watching her grow into the woman this valley has produced is absolutely amazing. Her faith is tenacious, her prayers are fervent, her spirit is vibrant, and her beauty is incomparable. I've watched my wife triumph over tremendous adversity and afflictions. The manner in which she trusts God is contagious. My wife is an absolute brainiac; this woman is sharp as a razor, very intelligent, which makes her more attractive. I am impressed with her intellect. I am sitting back in awe watching this brilliant woman enjoy life and seek after everything God has for her. My wife is my best friend and a proud occupant of my eagle's nest. I am excited to be a part of this group of "extraordinary eagles."

The greatest spoil I took from the valley is the newly found relationship and perspective I have toward God. I've been in a committed relationship with Jesus Christ now for over fifteen years, but I can honestly say just a few months ago did I obtain this truth in which I'm about to share. It's nothing new, and many of you, if not all you readers, might have arrived at this place a long time ago. I read "The Parable of the Prodigal Son" (also known as the Lost Son, Running Son, Loving Father, or Lovesick Father), which appears in Luke 15:11–32. The word *prodigal* means "wastefully extravagant." This son, as the story unfolds, asks for his inheritance, and after wasting his fortune, he becomes destitute and returns home. His intention is to beg his father to become one of his hired servants, expecting his relationship with his father likely to be severed. The father, when he sees his son coming from a distance, he runs toward him and embraces him so tightly while wrapping his arms around his neck. The son didn't expect such a reception, and not only that, the father had a big celebration in honor of his son who had come back home. He gave his son the best and treated him like royalty.

I now view God as my father who loves me in a greater capacity than I love my own children. In all of my days, I have never encountered a parent who doesn't want anything less than the best for their children. It doesn't matter how hurt or disappointed we can become because of some the mistakes our children make, but we never stop loving them. I remember when my oldest son, Bryan, turned down the opportunity to run track on a full scholarship, I was so disappointed. I couldn't believe he allowed his dreams to slip away like that, but then I came to myself. Was it really his dream, or the dream I had envisioned for him? The principle is this: I didn't stop loving him. My love grew stronger for him. I didn't outcast him. I embraced him even the more.

In the valley we tend to think for God, dictating how he will respond to our failures or lack of good decision making. God is not sitting on the throne waiting to punish us; he's just like the father of the prodigal son running toward us, waiting to embrace us and give us his best. We are royalty to God because we are his children. I don't identify with being a pastor or teacher. I identify with being a "child of God" who will make mistakes in this lifetime, endure valley experiences and storms, and run home to my father after I get up from the falls of life knowing that "He loves me anyway."

YOUR MOUNTAIN AWAITS YOU

"For you shall go out with joy and be led forth with peace: the mountains and the hills shall break forth before you into singing, and all the trees of the field shall clap their hands" (Isa. 55:12). In the context of this scripture, God is sending the children of Israel a fresh assurance of deliverance from Babylonian captivity.

> Weeping, we sat beside the rivers of Babylon thinking of Jerusalem, we have put away our lyres, hanging them upon the branches of the willow trees, for how can we sing, yet our captors, our tormentors, demand that we sing for them the happy songs of Zion, if I forget you, O Jerusalem, let my right hand forget its skill upon the harp. If I fail to love her more than my highest joy, let me never sing again. (Ps. 137:1–6)

This psalm gives us a little insight of how the children of Israel suffered as well as their spiritual disposition. It describes how they sat beside the rivers of Babylonian, weeping, crying. As tough as my valley experience was, and oftentimes I shed many tears, but not in a million years can I relate to what the children of Israel endured while in captivity. The psalm explains how their captors would torment them, demanding they sing happy songs of Zion. Zion was one of the hills on which Jerusalem stood. When King David brought the Ark to Zion, the hill became Sacred. Zion came to be used for the whole of Jerusalem, and the name is frequently used figuratively for the Jewish Church and for heaven. They were being tormented when commanded to sing happy songs of Zion. In this sense, the Babylonians thought that God had abandoned the children of Israel and would celebrate that idea. The Babylonians knew that the destruction of the temple and the exile to Babylon represents a tremendous shock to the Jewish people. In those days, it was normal for the Jewish people, "children of Israel," to live in the constant presence of God, which was always accessible at the temple. Miracles occurred there daily and could be witnessed by anyone. Happy songs of Zion were sung daily in the presence of the Lord at the temple. It was the Zenith of spirituality for the Jewish people.

But now in captivity, all of that is gone—the land, the joy, the temple, and God's presence. That's the reason why they wept by the rivers of Babylon. But relief is soon to come for the Jewish people. God encourages them with precious words of hope and vindication. In like manner, God sent me a fresh assurance of my impending deliverance from the captivity of my valley experience when He dropped in my spirit these words: "Your mountain awaits you."

It was the beginning of the year 2017, and my home state of Virginia had received a healthy dose of snow. Newport News, the city in which I live, received I believe six to ten inches. My family and I were held captive in our home for about three days, and on the fourth day, the sun arose, melting the ice and the snow. I must admit I'm not a huge fan of the snow, but

God put on a display of beauty as the snow blanketed our area. Everything seemed pure. I was at work the next morning when I noticed the sun beaming down on the snow and ice, and God spoke to me. He said, "In the same way the sun is shining on the snow and ice is how the son will be shining on your life." I drove maybe a mile down the road when God spoke the same words to me again, but this time, I was at a red light, and I could barely see through the window because the sun was shining so bright.

I immediately called my wife and told her about my encounter with God. For the past two years, I felt I was a prisoner to the valley with an undetermined sentence until the Lord led me to this particular chapter in the book of Isaiah. As I studied, seeking devotional application, God spoke. "I am releasing you from the valley, and your mountain awaits you. In the same manner I reassured Israel, I am reassuring you today." I understood something in that conversation that proved to be monumental, which answered one of my greatest concerns while in the valley. God had previously answered the question I had in reference to how I arrived at the valley. Everyone's entrance to their valley is different. That's why it's pivotal to stay in the presence of God, in the Word of God, even at your lowest because that's how you get all your concerns addressed and receive your strength. Scripture says in the presence of the Lord, there is fullness of joy. The children of Israel had no joy while in Babylon because they weren't in the presence of the Lord. It doesn't matter how bad your feel, how ashamed you feel, how confused you may be, how exhausted you are physically, mentally, or spiritually. Stay before the Lord. He is greater than your emotions.

In seeking the Lord for answers to how I arrived at my valley, God showed me how He had great faith in Job and yet mentioned him to Satan. Job endured his "Valley of Suffering" only to be blessed more than he had been before. Jehoshaphat, because he wouldn't compromise, walked (lived and relied) on the word of God. Jehoshaphat endured the "Battle in the Valley of Tekoa" only to become victorious and change the name to the "Valley of Blessing." Neither me Job or Jehoshaphat are perfect, especially me. I make mistakes every day and will continue to come short. I am human just like everyone else, but what I am saying is this: Don't automatically condemn yourselves in the valley because you think you've done something to deserve it.

God showed me in KJV ISAIAH verses 55:8–9: "For my thoughts are not your thoughts, neither are your ways my ways, saith the Lord, For as the heavens are higher than the earth, so are my ways higher than your ways, and my thoughts than your thoughts." Sometimes you will not be able to think your way through situations or find the solution to your problems or experiences, but just remember, God has a plan for your life, and trust in His ability to outthink you, understanding He only wants the best for you.

The reason I entered the valley is, simply put, it was a part of God's plan for my life. This valley experience was on God's GPS to my destiny, and without it, I wouldn't have arrived to the place where I am now. God sees the bigger picture. "Your Mountain awaits you." God is saying, "I'm bringing you out of your low place and into your place of exaltation. I'm taking you from the bottom to the top." God showed me in Isaiah 55:12 His supernatural power. He allowed me to see the mountains and hills singing, the trees clapping, celebrating my victory over the valley, awaiting my arrival. I thought of it as imagery, but God showed me the allegory, which means a deeper meaning. God wanted me to understand that He is able to do, exceeding abundantly above all that we ask or think according to the power that works in us.

On the mountain, things are going to manifest and happen beyond your wildest dreams and exceed your greatest expectations. Doors that were closed before will all of a sudden open. The things that God will release to you on the mountain doesn't even require the faith to receive it. You can't believe God for something you didn't even think of. If you could imagine it, then it would require you to exercise your faith to believe Him for it.

One day while working on my route, I walked into the patient accounting department to deliver the mail, just like any other day, but this time Mr. Chris Spady, now a good friend of mine and the manager of the department, asked me if I could come into his office for a second to speak with him. He wasn't my good friend as of yet, so I was nervous. Although he was very professional and polite, I thought I was in trouble. My initial thought was, *What in the world did you do, Domeka?* When I stepped into the office, Chris began to thank me for being so polite, cheerful, and helpful, and he told me that he really appreciated everything I was doing for his department. I was absolutely blown away. Here I was thinking I was in trouble for doing something wrong, but in his humility and kindness, he was thanking me. I didn't think I was contributing any more than anyone else. I was just doing my job, which I love to do, but then he further said, "Domeka, I don't really know what it is about you, but I sense there is something special about you. I appreciate how every day you come in greeting everyone, and even though it's for a short time, the time you're here makes a difference. Everyone here feels your presence and are motivated by it. Domeka, I don't know how to say it but I'm going to say it anyway."

Then he asked the million-dollar question: "What makes you smile?"

He added, "The reason I asked is because we have meetings here in the office, and everyone attends. We use these meetings as a time of motivation for the team, and I would love for you to come and speak to us all and tell us a little about you and the reason you smile all the time."

I agreed, and walked away thinking I had just spoken to the most pure, genuine human being the Lord had created. I thanked God for allowing someone like Chris to see Jesus in me, and I even cried a few tears of joy as I got back in my work van praising God. The entire day I was thinking, *Man, how in the world am I going to let the entire office know that Jesus Christ is the reason I smile without overstepping boundaries in the workplace?* Chris had already made the statement in his office that he had an idea why I smiled. I knew he was a believer; it permeated all through him. I'm so glad God is omniscient, all knowing, because he read my mind.

The next day Chris informed me he had spoken to my supervisor and was made aware I'm a pastor. I asked Chris was it still okay, and he said absolutely. I was excited to have a platform in the marketplace. The engagement was phenomenal. I incorporated the mission of our company, Riverside, into my speech. I became completely immersed into this opportunity. I prepared as if I was studying for a sermon. I believe in representing Jesus Christ with a spirit of excellence. The mission statement of Riverside Hospital is "to care for others as we would we care for those we love, and to enhance their well-being and improve their health." The mission became my mission. Chris wanted me to explain to everyone the reason I smiled. I explained to them that ultimately, Jesus is the reason I smile, but being able to work with such great coworkers and being a part of a company that's making a difference is another reason why I smile. Chris wanted me to bring some inspiration and motivation; therefore, I decided to share with them the meaning of our clothing brand Egeiro. *Egeiro* is a Greek word meaning "to arise, to arouse from sleep, to awake, to recall the dead to life, to raise up, stir up, to build, to produce." It's from the idea of a person gathering their faculties or, in other words, getting themselves together. Our brand Egeiro is inspired by the teachings of Jesus Christ.

In the book of John 5, Jesus sees through His eyes of compassion an impotent (unable to take effective action, helpless, or powerless) man who was in that condition for thirty-eight years, lying down on his bed by the side of a pool that provided healing when an angel came at a particular season or time to stir the water, and whoever stepped into the water first became healed of whatever disease they had. Jesus asked the man did he want to be healed. The man replied with an excuse. He said, "Sir, I have no one to put me into the pool when the water is stirred. Therefore, someone steps into the water before I do." Jesus responded, "Egeiro (arise) pick up your bed and walk." Instantly the man was healed and empowered to pick up his bed and walk. The man was now able to "get up, get over it, and get going." Henry Ford said, "When everything seems to be going against you just remember the airplane doesn't take off with the wind, it takes off against the wind." Egeiro inspires people to overcome their circumstances or situations regardless of how difficult they may seem. Jesus by faith can make an impotent person potent (having great power, influence, or effect). Egeiro is not just an article or garment of clothing we wear; it's a mindset we put on.

The engagement went so well that Chris asked me to speak at another engagement, but this time it was more important with a lot more people along with a little added pressure because he explained to me that the company was now transitioning to another system, and he had to address some very important issues that may leave some people a little discouraged and in need for motivation, and I didn't have the security of my Bible in front of me with a church congregation shouting "Amen!" giving me support, so I was definitely out of my element on this one.

The engagement turned out to be perfect, and God's timing of the engagement was even more perfect. The company transitioning to another system paralleled my valley experience. Thanks to Chris's precise and detailed teaching of the new system, I was able to pinpoint some of the benefits and gather enough information to understand why indeed the company was moving into its current direction and that for a short while, his staff would have to sacrifice with maybe longer days while enduring a learning curve that would benefit them in the future, among other sacrifices they would make. I was amazed when he introduced me. They had my name in large letters glaring from the projection screen in a room filled with what I call corporate America. I was so nervous, but I knew God would seize the moment. The purpose for this engagement was similar to the book *Victory in the Valley*. Therefore during the ice breaker, I quoted our company's mission statement: "We care for others as we would care for those we love." I then asked everyone in the room to shout "We care!" It was a very powerful moment. It felt like the Holy Spirit filled the room, that's the Riverside way. The message was very simple, about fifteen minutes long, and I explained they were in the "Valley of Epic" similar to my valley experience. Epic is the name of the system they were transitioning to and that the Valley of Epic wasn't designed to defeat them; it was just a temporary holding place preparing them for the "Mountain of Epic." I further encouraged them that the adversity would surely turn into triumph. Colin Powell said, "A dream doesn't become reality through magic, it takes sweat, determination, and hard work." The difficult road they were about to embark on would lead them to an expected end where Epic would be everything they envisioned it to be. I concluded with a little of my testimony, which bought me and almost everyone present to tears, along with a phrase that I coined, "We are Riversidians," which would secure our success while in the Valley of Epic. A Riversidian isn't just a normal employee working for a paycheck, but a citizen of Riverside, someone who has adopted the mission of the company as their own, and a major benefit of being a citizen is that you're a part of a community, and communities rally together and fight for whatever the cause is at hand. Concluding that Riversidians would embrace the challenges of the "Valley of Epic," progressing together all the way to the "Mountaintop of Epic."

This is an example of God doing something, exceeding what I could even ask or think. God opening doors to opportunities I hadn't even dreamed about, which wouldn't require me to exercise my faith. I am confident now. God is calling me into motivational speaking, and I am excited to be able to walk into everything He has for me. On the mountain God will send His *Shaar*, Hebrew word for "gatekeeper" (gatekeepers are those who open doors to the entrances of your destiny). Chris Spady is a *shaar* (gatekeeper that God used to open this door to an entrance into my destiny). It is amazing to see God use people in extraordinary ways when they don't have any inclination to the fact God is using them, yielding to the leading of the spirit of God. Scripture says, "The steps of a good man are ordered by the Lord and he delight in his way."

A year prior, my supervisor, Mr. Bud Proctor, who also is a *shaar* for the Lord, emphatically convinced me to change my route. He wanted me to leave the route I drove the past three years, prompting me to leave people who I had grown comfortable with like family. I tried to maneuver and find a way out of it, and normally it would work. Mr. Bud and I have a great working relationship and friendship, but the more I begged him to allow me to stay on my current route, the sterner he became. I finally realized he wasn't going to bend when he said, "Domeka, you have no other choice. I need you on this route." He's the boss, so I eventually accepted the fact I was venturing off to something new. The last day I drove my old route, I cried because I was so disappointed I had to leave my friends behind, but to my surprise, the first day on my new route, I quickly fell in love with it. Ms. Diane and Ms. Melinda Deal at the wellness center from day one became my new best friends at Riverside, greeting me with the biggest smiles and saying they heard great things about me and that they looked forward to meeting me. This was the beginning of many confirmations I would receive, allowing me to know God was in control. I now understand why Mr. Bud Proctor was unwavering in his approach in changing my route. God was using him, and without him, I wouldn't have been introduced to Chris Spady, and without Chris Spady, I wouldn't discover the next phase of my destiny.

I was finishing up the book, working on the last chapter, when I ran into I guess the term would be a "writer's block." From the beginning of this book, whenever I sat down and became committed to write, the Lord would pour out His words to me as a flowing river. I told my wife I was having trouble finishing the book, and she said, "Maybe God has more for you to experience before you can conclude it." Sure enough, she was correct. God's *shaar* Steve Barrs, weeks prior to me reaching the last chapter of the book, invited me to attend the Commonwealth Prayer Breakfast, which is absolutely powerful. Each year, many of Virginia's elected government leaders gather with citizens from throughout the Commonwealth to reaffirm our trust in God, recognize His reconciling power, and seek his guidance. It was very informative and encouraging for someone like me who doesn't know a great deal about politics, who only looks from the outside in. I feel strong and proud to be a Native Virginian, seeing the measures that are being taken by the leaders in our state, inviting and welcoming God through prayer, asking for his guidance. I had the opportunity to be in the same room with some very influential and important people such as the Honorable Terry McAuliffe, Governor of Virginia; the Honorable Levar Stoney, mayor, city of Richmond; Gabe Lyons, author and founder of Q, just to name a few. I was moved deeply by the Honorable Paul Trible, president of Christopher Newport University. I could listen to him speak on the behalf of Christ all day long. The Honorable Mark Herring, attorney general of Virginia, read scripture. I was moved to tears by the passionate prayers of the Honorable Rosalyn Dance, Senate of Virginia, and the Honorable Dietra Trent, secretary of education. The whole while I was there, God reminded me, "Your mountain awaits you." At one point, I had to step away from everyone just to ask God what was my purpose of being there. He responded, "A man's gift maketh room for him, and bringeth him before great men" (Prov. 18:16). My spirit led me to stand at one side of the room just so I could look across the room to see the enormous size of this room filled with hundreds of great men and women. God repeated, "Your gift make room for you. This is just the beginning of what I have in store for you."

I was born and raised in downtown Newport "Bad" News, where its believed "nothing good can come from out of the hood." I have many friends who have overcome that sentiment, becoming successful lawyers, teachers, city officials, authors, entrepreneurs, college graduates, pastors, parents, mentors, professional athletes. But never in a million years did I think it could happen for me. I was in the same room with people who I normally would only see in the courtrooms or TV, but today, I was their guest. I sat in awe of everything that was transpiring. Gabe Lyons, who I follow on Instagram, now I was in the same room hearing him personally as he poured out his heart.

The moment had arrived when I took out my phone to snap some pictures of everything going on around me. I wanted to savor the moment, but my spirit spoke to me in my wife's voice, saying, "Act like you've been here before. Get used to this because God is enlarging your territory." I put my phone back in my pocket, sat up in my seat, and smiled. God was giving me a glimpse into my future. All I could do was just look at my brother Steve Barrs in amazement, thinking how great God had used him today to add to my book and destiny.

Sometimes God will allow people to see in you what you don't see in yourself. "Your mountain awaits you." All I can think about is I'm still climbing up the side of the mountain. I haven't made it to the top yet, and God is raining blessings on my life. I understand on the side of the mountain, God will allow you to build "mountain relationships" with people who don't know where you come from but can perceive purpose in you and will assist in any fashion they can. The Commonwealth Prayer Breakfast, which was held at the Greater Richmond Convention Center, was a part of God's plan for me—another example of God doing exceeding above anything I ask or think, which didn't require me to exercise my faith. It was the Grace of God that brought me to that moment. I didn't deserve it and couldn't earn it.

As I continued to reflect on Isaiah 55:12 and God sending me a fresh assurance of my deliverance from captivity of my valley experience, one of my dreams became a reality.

Wherefore seeing we also are compassed about
with so great a cloud of witnesses, let us lay
aside every weight, and the sin which doth so
easily beset us, and let us run with patience
the race that is set before us. (Heb. 12:1)

It wasn't just the mountains and hills singing and the trees celebrating by clapping their hands; there is a cloud of witnesses in heaven cheering you on as well. The entire host of heaven is looking down while you're in the valley, cheering and strengthening you through it all. Every day while at my lowest, I felt the presence of my grandmother (Shirley Kelley) and Trina Fullwood (my mother-in-law) rooting me on, telling me not to give up, that I could make it. The principle is this: There are more people that are for you than those that are against you. You have people that are interceding for you right now that are in the very presence of God. Isaiah 55:12 says, "That you will go out with joy and be led forth with peace." Although the valley is difficult, discouraging, draining you emotionally, physically, spiritually, and mentally, according to this scripture, you take joy and peace with you. Joy and peace are not gained on the mountain. God gives you joy and peace in the midst of the valley (your lowest). It is so awesome to know that in the midst of the difficulties while in the valley, God blesses us with peace and joy where with we don't have to wait for our circumstances to change before the peace and joy come. Isaiah 26:3 says, "Thou wilt keep him in perfect peace whose mind is stayed on thee, because he trusteth in thee."

In my conclusion to *Victory in the Valley*, God answered a very important question for me, which I discovered in Psalm 102:13: "Thou shalt arise, and have mercy upon Zion, for the time to favor her, yea, the set time, is come." God will not share his glory with no one. God had to separate and severe many relationships, and oftentimes I didn't understand why God was moving in that direction, but it was completely out of my control. I found myself questioning God. In bringing you to your destiny, God doesn't want anyone feeling as if they were the determining factor, although they may have been instrumental. On your mountain, no one can take credit for the mighty works of the Hand of God. This is the appointed time for God to favor you according to this scripture, the set time is come, and God has an appointed time in everything that He does.

Habakkuk 2:3 says, "For the vision is yet for an appointed time, but at the end it shall speak, and not lie, though it tarry wait for it because it will surely come." I encouraged myself by reminding myself of these promises. It didn't matter how long I was going to stay in the valley. I knew that the vision God showed me would surely come to pass and speak, declaring the favor and goodness of God. What God has promised you is going to speak for you.

In John 11:21, Martha said in reference to her brother Lazarus's death, "If you had been here, my brother had not died." Jesus four days later came and rose Lazarus from death to life. Jesus wanted Martha to understand that His timing was perfect. He didn't come when she wanted him to; He came when she thought it was all over. There will be times in the valley when doors will close, opportunities all but perish away, hope seems to dwindle, but then all of a sudden, God shows up, making all things beautiful. God's timing is perfect. He shows up big on our behalf. Martha had faith in Jesus. She knew He could heal Lazarus, but Jesus wanted to show up big on Martha's behalf. He wanted to do something greater than a healing; therefore, he performed a resurrection. "God's desire is to change our perspective. There is a danger in small thinking. As long as you think small, you will remain small, but when you understand

God is a Big God that does Big Things, you no longer limit God with pint-size prayers."

I had to endure my valley experience so God could break out of the box I had enclosed Him in. Jesus taught Martha a valuable lesson about life, which I now apply to my daily life. Jesus told Martha that he was the resurrection and the life, and anyone who believes in Him should never die, and he asked her, "Do you believe what I just told you?" Martha responded, "I do."

Anastasis is a Greek word for *resurrection*, which means "a raising up, restored to life, a standing up again." Jesus in this story used Lazarus as a representation of the many Christians who have the opportunity to enjoy life in him but yet are dead, enduring life instead of enjoying it. Jesus told Martha that in essence, you don't have to die in order to live, so live life to its absolute fullest. Martha thought she knew that Lazarus was going to rise or live again at the resurrection, but Jesus said, "No. Live now, I am the resurrection."

Pre-valley, I wasn't enjoying life. I thought my joy was connected to what I had instead of who I had. I lived without seeking the purposes and meaning of each day. I placed more value on one day more than the next. I would often look forward to Friday, Saturday, and Sunday, missing what God had for me Monday through Thursday. I bought me a "Significant Day" notebook where I keep track of every significant event I encountered on a daily basis. Now life for me has become more purposeful. Cherish and honor the people God has placed in your life. Don't allow a day to go by without telling them how much you love them and how much you care. Those were the words I spoke to my youngest son, Malik, after he told me one of his friend's five-year-old brother went home to be with the

Lord. Malik said, "Dad, I now understand what it means to live every day as if it was your last."

Jesus also showed Martha when he provided a resurrection instead of healing was the fact that God can and will show up big on her behalf in a new way. God told the children of Israel through the prophet Isaiah, "But forget all that, remember not the former things it is nothing compared to what I'm going to do, for I'm going to do a brand new thing. See, I have already begun, don't you see it, I will make a road through the wilderness of the world for my people to go home and create rivers for them in the desert." I learned when the doors of the church closed that God was simply doing a new thing, and I had to accept His plan. God made a way for us in the wilderness and created rivers in the desert, so to speak. I was comfortable with a small church, but God's plan is much bigger than that. He has a worldwide plan for Psalms, and yes, one of my biggest dreams became a reality. I now can say that Liberty Baptist is my church, a church with a world mission, and I serve under Pastor Grant and his wife, Ms. Tammy. I am a part of their Leadership Team, and our ministries have partnered together for the Kingdom.

God is moving in a new way. I was able to serve at an event called "Acts of Love," where Liberty brings in retired NFL football players such as my favorite, Keith Davis, a powerful passionate man of God, who played for the Super Bowl–winning New York Giants, where they present the Gospel in a unique and powerful way. I witnessed hundreds of people being saved and immediately baptized. The spirit of God was moving in ways I never experienced before. The service was pure as the Love of Jesus Christ flowed throughout. I had the opportunity to tag along with First Lady Ms. Tammy as she went up and down, back and forth, throughout the church, looking in excitement for someone to welcome and thank them for attending the service. Her love for people is contagious. If you stay around her long enough, you will catch hold of it. I was amazed.

I was in the green room with my pastor, Pastor Grant, a man who, throughout the years, has mentored me from a distance, and now I was there up close and personal as he was preparing to speak. He kneeled down in prayer, submitting to the Lord, thanking God for the opportunity. I was observing, filled with joy. I couldn't believe I was in the midst of it all. Being in the presence of Pastor Grant, you know that Jesus is in the room with you. Pastor Grant has a determination to lead as many to Jesus as he possibly can; he genuinely cares for everyone he encounters. In the sanctuary, he called me up to the pulpit with him, and I was almost blinded by the lights and the cameras. He introduced me to everyone in sanctuary as his brother and the pastor of Psalms Ministries, who Liberty was now partnering with.

When I tell you I have never felt so much love inside one place with so many people there at the same time, I was speechless. It was as if I was in a dream, not wanting to wake up. The voice of Joel Osteen was echoing in my head: "With one move of God he can take you from the back to the front of the line. He can make you the head and not the tail." When you think it's all over, God is simply doing something new. I don't know what God has in store for Psalms and Liberty, but I can assure you it's something "exceeding above and beyond what I can think, ask, or even imagine."

You will have to wait and see in the sequel book, *Moments on the Mountain*. I thank Pastor Grant, Ms. Tammy, and Liberty Baptist for believing in me while I was in my valley, and people's belief in me always encouraged me to give it my best shot, and that is what I intend to do.

My sister called me the other day feeling a little down. Her heart was heavy. She went on to say that she had been praying to God on my behalf because during my valley experience, I would always tell her that I was fine, but she needed reassurance from God. While in the shower, she said God spoke to her these words: "Don't worry about your brother, he is fine. He is a man of faith like Abraham. I will make his name great." My sister, April "Lucy Bell" Kelley said she continued to pray, making sure she was hearing from God alone and that it wasn't her flesh or hopeful thinking. Then suddenly, a peace came upon her concerning me. She called me with such confidence and excitement, knowing that our lives and ministry would change forever.

My wife and I were riding home from work one day, and we were talking about all the adversity we had endured the past two years and how God remained faithful. My wife uttered the words of Apostle Paul, "These troubles and sufferings of ours are, after all, are quite small and won't last very long, yet this short time of distress will result in God's richest blessings upon us forever and ever." What we endured made us stronger, brought our entire family closer, and God has already begun the restoration process.

I had a meeting with the mortgage company, who offered the building back to us, willing to work out favorable terms but not being anxious for anything. We are currently praying about it with the understanding that God has something greater in store for us "Dream Bigger." You will have to read the sequel, *Moments on the Mountain*, to see the move of God, which will be available soon in every place where a book can be sold.

God has restored many relationships in my life with people who were always there loving me unconditionally. God has even given us new friends who celebrate us and are happy with what God is doing with my family. God has restored us spiritually, mentally, and financially. Life is good because God is good. I am growing as a pastor, having the opportunity to learn and humble myself under a great pastor and teacher in Pastor Grant. I am currently working in the master's program, pursuing my dream to teach and become a professor at a Christian university. I was offered a position to coach basketball at the high school level, but you will have to read the sequel, *Moments on the Mountain*, to see where God is taking us.

I learned in the valley that not everyone is going to agree with what God is doing with your life, but you cannot be consumed with the people on the sidelines watching your race. You have to run your own, become everything you want to do. Deacon Willie "String Bean" Mack once told me, "Pastor, when you set one bar, reach it, and then set another higher, and don't ever stop setting bars." Deacon Todd Wharton encouraged me greatly in my valley, saying, "Pastor, only if the world knew where you came from, they would appreciate where you're going." He said, "Continue to write, Pastor."

I am now officially an author, and I owe it all to the valley. Throughout my valley experience, I often asked God how long will this last and how do I know when I ascend to my mountain. He responded, "Don't rush the valley, the valley isn't designed to defeat you. It's a temporary holding place preparing you for the mountain." I received my answer in the definition of a mountain. A mountain is "a large natural elevation of the earth's surface rising abruptly from the surrounding level." I didn't and you won't have to look for anything supernatural to take place in your life elevating you to your mountain. Things are going to happen right where you are, naturally and abruptly. It's simply the Grace of God, His *charis* unearned, unmerited, the good will and loving-kindness of God.

A great friend of my mine, the very talented Calvin Wright, said it best: "You just have to trust the process." Dick Woodward illustrated grace in this way. Whenever his children would go out and come home late after being involved in whatever they would be, he had two signs posted up, one at the bottom of the stairs hanging above, strategically placed there so they could read it. It had the words "God loves you anyway," and at the top of the stairs, another sign read, "And I love you anyway." The valley isn't designed to defeat you. It's a temporary holding place preparing you for the mountain. Champions aren't produced on the mountain; they are celebrated there, and victors not victims are prepared in the valley. Your mountain awaits you.

CPSIA information can be obtained
at www.ICGtesting.com
Printed in the USA
FFOW03n1348030318
45351396-46019FF